MASTERS OF
ANIMATION
JOHN HALAS

MASTERS OF ANIMATION

JOHN HALAS

SALEM HOUSE PUBLISHERS
TOPSFIELD, MASSACHUSETTS

First published in the United States
by Salem House Publishers 1987
462 Boston Street, Topsfield, MA 01983

Library of Congress Cataloging in Publication Data

Halas, John.
Masters of animation.

Includes index.
1. Animation (Cinematography)—History.
I Title.
TR897.5.H335 1987 778.5′347′09 87–4865
ISBN 0–88162–306–7

Set in Monophoto Bembo and printed in Great Britain
by Jolly & Barber Ltd, Rugby, Warwickshire
Bound by Butler & Tanner Ltd, Frome and London

CONTENTS

PREFACE

This book accompanies (and, indeed, expands upon) a television series of the same name. I am grateful to both BBC TV and BBC Books for taking up the project with such enthusiasm.

Inevitably, the 'masters of animation' presented here are only a very few of the animators around the world who deserve mention, it would be impossible to do justice to them all. I would therefore like to express my regrets to those who have been excluded, and my thanks to all the friends and colleagues who kindly submitted their work for selection: especially to the members of the International Animated Film Association; the National Film Board of Canada; the Canadian Broadcasting Corporation; Zagreb Animated Film Studio, Yugoslavia; Soyuzmultfilm, Moscow; Pannonia Studio, Hungary, and the Disney Studio in California. I would also like to mention the following individuals for their help in the production of the series: Leo Salkin in the USA; Osvaldo Cavandoli in Italy; Ivica Njers in Yugoslavia; Gerry Potterton and Mike Mills in Canada, and John Coates and Bob Godfrey in England.

Further thanks are extended to Pat Webb, for assisting me in research and for typing the manuscript so diligently, to designer Linda Blakemore and to Talia Rodgers, who patiently and skilfully edited the text.

John Halas, London, 1986

INTRODUCTION

From the very beginning of cinematography, moving pictures were admirably placed to visually express new ideas and explore technical innovations. Consequently, these two aspects developed simultaneously: their progress is traced in Part One of this book. Today, they are still closely interrelated and, to some extent, dependent on each other for the further development of animated film.

Animated cartoons attempt to recreate graphically physical or organic movement. Unlike live-action film, however, animation has the greater flexibility of using motion creatively. That is to say, it can exaggerate physical possibilities by slowing movement down, speeding it up and using it comically or expressively. Herein lies the starting point of the art of animation.

We are all familiar with animated cartoons as mass entertainment, especially for children. Television has provided universal exposure for this type of cartoon animation and it seems that there is no end to the demand for it. There are also, however, many examples of animation's potential for communicating witty visual ideas and sophisticated narratives to older audiences; some animated films not only have immediate appeal but are memorable and contain interesting social comment.

Educational animation for both children and adults is even more under-used. In this category the medium becomes a new language, using images far more wide-ranging than the world of mice and rabbits. Unfortunately many still think of that as the extent of animated cartoons. Moving lines, colours, shapes and symbols can represent the essence of an idea or an emotion, and can express it with clarity, force or humour. With animation, ideas can be expressed using only a fraction of the time needed with conventional teaching methods. This form of visual education could be significantly expanded for the overall benefit of our society. Today we find that, while the scope of animation has developed to a considerable extent, its use lags badly behind: its main arenas are still advertising and children's entertainment. It has long been felt that this is too limiting for a medium with such vast potential.

A further drawback for animation is that it still lacks serious critical appreciation. Compared with other media such as the fine arts, cinema or music, animation is, by and large, a badly neglected form. It has few critics who are able to analyse what is good or bad, or who know what values to look for in an animated film. Many make the mistake of comparing animation with live-action productions, making unfair comparisons between two very different disciplines. Moreover, general audiences have only been exposed to one type of animation, that of popular, funny, and usually American, cartoons, as if there were only 'pop' music and no other kind. In Part Two, an attempt is made to prove that, throughout the history of the medium, a great number of works have emerged from all over the world which deserve proper attention from the critics and greater appreciation by the general public. These works contain a great deal of dramatic power, sophistication, satire, poetry, and pictorial effects, many of which can only be conveyed through animation.

In the third and final section there is a look at how, with the aid of new technologies, animation is very much in the forefront of the development of a contemporary art movement, leaving behind other arts which do not utilise such novel elements as computer-generated motion, electronic pictures, sound effects, synthesised music and special effects.

Admittedly, animation is, relatively speaking, something of a newcomer, both to the Arts and to visual communication in general. There is no reason, however, why it should not be used more effectively, especially in interpreting or explaining the complex structure of our society and the new discoveries of a technologically-orientated society, eager for information, knowledge and amusement.

PART ONE

THE MEDIUM

THE MECHANICS OF MOVING PICTURES

It would be misleading to suggest that animation, as a genre, has a history of its own. Inextricably bound up with both the study of optics and the development of cinematography, animation itself has been 'invented' so many times by so many different individuals that its true starting point could be placed almost anywhere.

In attempting to understand the basis of animated pictures, however, the first aspect to be considered is the physiological factor known as 'persistence of vision'. This phenomenon occurs because the retina of the human eye retains the image of an object for a brief instant after the object has been removed from view. A series of still pictures presented in rapid sequence will therefore blend into a continuous image. This illusion was first detected thousands of years ago, notably by the early Egyptians who developed it in the form of children's toys.

Another early contributor to this field of study was Roger Bacon, an English monk in the thirteenth century. Bacon was a classical scholar and the first to analyse the optical effect of shadows. Friar Bacon was regarded by most of his contemporaries as a mad monk who played with magic and the 'powers of darkness', but his immense contribution to human knowledge is now appreciated and understood. As far as motion pictures are concerned, his most interesting work is contained in his letter on 'The Power of Art and Nature and the Inefficiency of Magic'. In it he spoke of 'wonderful devices' to be found in the future: flying machines; self-propelled vehicles; underwater craft; lenses; microscopes and telescopes. He devoted some ten years to the study of optics: the concentration of rays and the principle of focus (necessary for picture projection) were both familiar to him. He recognised that light had a quantifiable speed; up to that time it had been thought that the speed of light was infinite. He also studied optical illusions pertaining to movement which are fundamental to the motion picture. Bacon is often cited as the inventor of the 'camera obscura' (although the Arabian scholar Alhazen actually described one 250 years earlier).

Above: an eighteenth-century engraving of a camera obscura

The concept behind the camera obscura dates back to antiquity, with Aristotle's description of how light waves behave when projected through a small aperture. What Bacon did was develop that into a large darkened room with a small circular opening in one wall through which light is shone into the room. An inverted image of the scene outside appears on the opposite wall, and, in its simplest form, the modern box camera is that room in miniature.

To Bacon must go the credit for one of the earliest descriptions of a camera used for scientific purposes. He wrote in his *Perspectiva*:

> 'Mirrors can be so arranged that, as often as we wish, any object, either in the house or the street, can be made to appear. Spectators looking at the image formed by the mirrors will see something real, but when they go to the place where the object seems to be, they will find nothing. For the mirrors are so cleverly arranged in relation to the object that the

images appear to be in space, formed there by the union of the visible rays. And the spectators will run to the place of the apparitions where they think the object actually is, but will find nothing but an illusion of the object.'

Bacon's assertion that, through the use of mirrors, objects are made to appear where they are not, certainly reminds one of the illusion of the modern motion picture. Bacon died in 1292 and today, nearly 700 years later, we consider him to be one of the founders of the history of light and shadow. His studies of lenses, mirrors and light effects, his speculative thinking and his practical experiments, laid the foundation for scientific research in modern optics.

Two centuries later, in the Renaissance climate of strong interest in visual accuracy and beauty, it was found that a portable 'camera' was a useful aid to drawing and painting from nature. Leone Battista Alberti, a notable architect of that period in Florence, was using a form of camera obscura for his scientific studies, but according to Vasari, the Renaissance historian, it was Leonardo da Vinci who took the camera obscura a step further as a practical instrument. He is reputed to have used the device to study and measure the reflection of light and perspective. Vasari refers to the fact that, like Bacon, Leonardo studied mirror reflections and how images were formed. He also studied the human eye and used the camera to establish principles of the mechanism of seeing. Leonardo da Vinci's greatest contribution to the evolution of motion pictures was undoubtedly his theoretical application of how to use the camera in relation to the human eye. The pinhole box camera was almost ready for others to turn into a successful device which could be explored in subsequent centuries.

It was, of course, at the beginning of the nineteenth century that the time was right for a great number of inventors to lead the world towards the discovery of stop-motion photography and the creation of frame-by-frame film animation. By the middle of the century the big race to create an illusion of motion through individual pictures was underway. The road was full of disappointments, brilliant inventions, patents, even law suits. The field eventually became so crowded with scientists, entrepreneurs and show business personalities that to this day it is difficult to assess the true importance of their contributions. What follows is an attempt at providing a coherent and selective sequence of events leading up to the widespread application of electrical power.

In 1825, Dr John Ayrton Paris put his 'Thaumatrope' on sale. This device, which became famous as a scientific plaything, was a disc of card with a picture of a bird on one side and a birdcage on the other. When the disc was twirled by means of strings attached to opposite edges, the viewer's eye retained the image of one side as the other side was revealed; the result was that the two images were superimposed – the bird appeared to be in the cage.

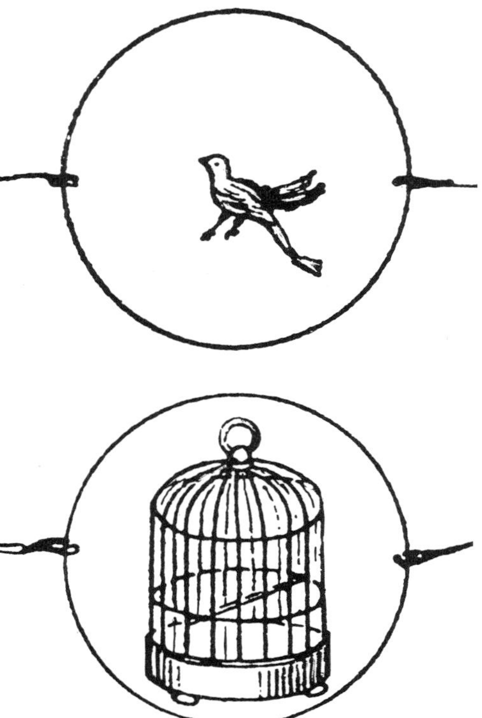

Above: Dr John Ayrton Paris' Thaumatrope (1825), showing both sides of the circular card

In 1832, a Belgian physicist called Joseph Plateau invented the Phenakistoscope, a revolving paper disc which had a number of figures pictured in different stages of movement spaced around it. When viewed through a mirror, they appeared to be one moving image. Similar inventions followed. In Austria, Simon Ritter von Stampfer produced *his* spinning discs to show motion, and in Britain, William George Horner devised a mechanical system which enabled several people to view the discs instead of just one individual.

In 1834, William Henry Fox Talbot began photographic investigations which were to lead to the permanent recording of the images of the 'camera obscura', and in 1838, Wheatstone invented the Stereoscope, giving the illusion of three-dimensional pictures by presenting two slightly different images.

In 1840, H. L. Childe adapted a magic lantern system with glass plates to produce what he called 'dissolving views'. Seven years later a turning point was reached when Niepce de Saint-Victor in France and Fox Talbot in Britain both began developing negative photographic images from a glass surface into positive images on paper. (This became especially significant later, when a photographic image had to be reproduced in picture-to-picture continuity and the original negative image stored for further use.)

It was not until 1861, however, that Coleman Sellers (an American) achieved a major breakthrough when he patented his 'Kinematoscope', a stereoscopic viewer using a paddle-wheel action to project continuous motion, and arguably the first actual photographic animation device.

Another important pioneer in the field was Eadweard Muybridge, an English-born American, famous for his analytical experiments which began in 1872. Possibly the best-known of them was in 1880 when he laid twenty-four still cameras linked to trip wires across a race track. When a horse broke through each wire as it ran, it triggered off the camera shutters, thereby taking a picture with every step. This succession of images showed the mechanics of movement in time with penetrating insight, and they are still in use today as a basis for studying the timing and character of human and animal movement, frame by frame.

One of Muybridge's more important contemporaries working in Europe was Emile Reynaud. A showman, inventor and artist, Reynaud was determined to improve the commercially exploited toys based on the 'persistence of vision' principle. So far, all the systems required the public to peep through rotating slits in order to watch the moving images: in 1877, Reynaud reversed the system. He used a circular cluster of revolving mirrors to reflect the drawings, which were on a horizontal band placed around the revolving drum. This time the onlookers were not required to look through anything, but could instead sit back and watch a relatively smooth moving picture projected via a series of mirrors. He called the contraption a 'Praxinoscope'.

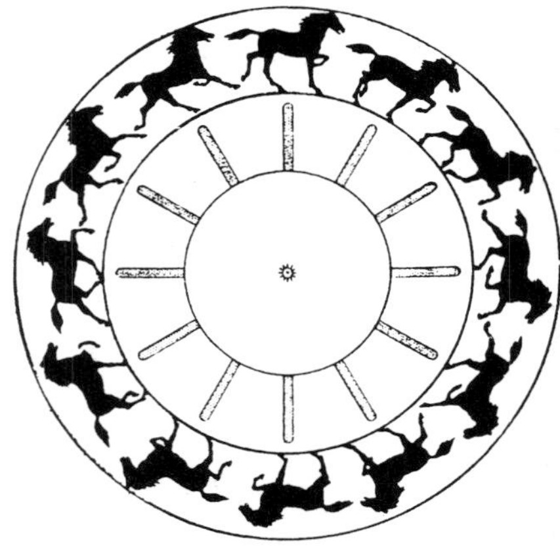

Above: Joseph Plateau's Phenakistoscope (1832), a development on the 'persistence of vision' principle. Plateau's invention inspired many other devices, including William George Horner's Zoetrope (below)

Above right: *Animal Locomotion* by Eadweard Muybridge (1887); right and far right: Emile Reynaud and his projecting Praxinoscope

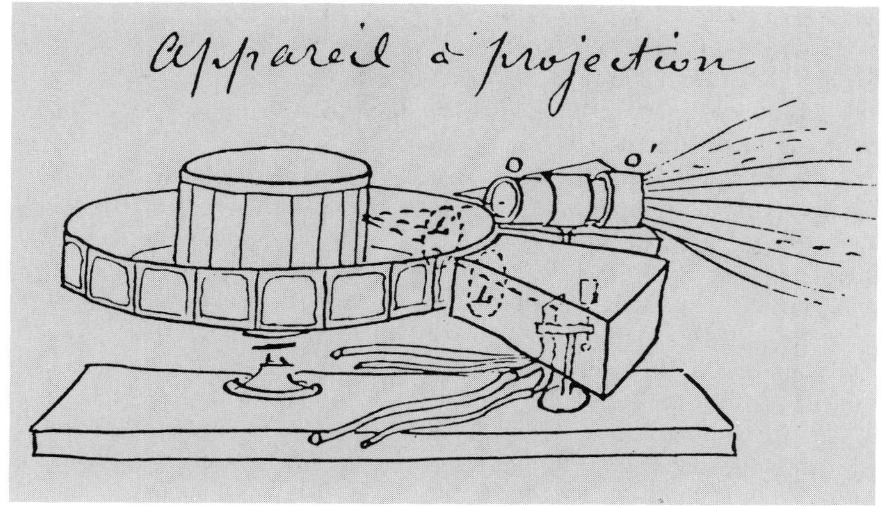
Appareil à projection

Above: Emile Reynaud's celebrated Théâtre Optique (1892)

By 1892, the apparatus had evolved into his 'Théâtre Optique', first presented at the Musée Grévin. This larger, more elaborate version could be viewed by a big audience and could last up to fifteen minutes. The projection took place from the rear onto a screen by means of a mirror and lens system, the actual images having been handpainted onto long strips of transparent celluloid. In order to keep the pictures steady, Reynaud punched holes onto the centre of the celluloid strips which were kept in register with a metal claw as they rotated along in a loop format. (The use of celluloid in animation was once again introduced some years later in New York by Earl Hurd, who patented his system in 1914. Today, animators still use his method of dividing a scene up into its component parts and painting each one onto a separate sheet of transparent material.)

Meanwhile, in 1887, Etienne-Jules Marey had come onto the scene in France with his experiments into the movement of abstract shapes photographed in colour onto glass plates. The manipulation of these shapes both fascinated the public and had a scientific application in the study of optics.

At around this time, Friese-Greene and Mortimer Evans were developing their 'box projector', which was capable of showing four to five frames per second. By the end of the nineteenth century, the American public was more than ready for an improved, popular form of moving picture show. The fairgrounds were full and for a nickel, one could look through a viewing slot and watch a film lasting a few seconds.

Auguste and Louis Lumière successfully projected live-action motion pictures onto a screen with their Cinématographe in March 1895, to a scientific society in Paris. The same event was publicly presented at

Top: Edison's Kinetoscope parlour in San Francisco (1894); above: engraving of Auguste Lumière demonstrating the Lumière Cinématographe in Paris (1895)

Marlborough Hall in Regent Street, London, the following year. Their invention owed much to the work of their predecessors (especially Muybridge and Marey), and managed to combine the apparatus of a camera with that of a projector. They are often regarded as the earliest actual film-makers, able to exhibit animated photographs of real people doing everyday things. Their first film was called *La Sortie des Usines Lumière*, and showed workers leaving the Lumière factory at the end of the day.

For quite a long time, however, there was very little real distinction in the public's mind between live-action film and animated drawings or paintings. The essence of both was *movement* and the idea of moving shadows and pictures on a screen was enough to enthral audiences throughout Europe and the USA. It was only when specialisation took place that the real differences in direction emerged. There were three strands forming at this time: straight cinema (referred to as 'live-action' film); animated films and cartoons (using the 'stop-motion' technique of photographing each stage of movement separately); and trick photography, which combined the two main strands and was live-action film with animated optical effects added.

The work of Georges Méliès, beginning in the 1890s, was an important step in the popularisation of these various forms of cinematography. Méliès was primarily a showman who astutely recognised the value of moving pictures as an entertainment medium. His films *Voyage to the Moon* (1902) and *The Conquest of The Pole* (1912) used special effects with superimposition and dissolves and his stories aptly pursued revelations of the impossible and the surreal. By today's standards, of course, they appear

Above: Georges Méliès' *Voyage to the Moon* (1902); above right: the opening title and two frames from Stuart Blackton's influential film *Humorous Phases of Funny Faces* (1906)

naïve and simplistic, but at the time they provided an exhilarating experience for his followers. His work undoubtedly influenced his contemporaries, Emile Reynaud and, later, Emile Cohl.

Meanwhile, in Britain, Arthur Melbourne Cooper had come up with what is often considered to be the world's first animated commercial. It was a stop-motion film of 'moving matchsticks' reputed to have been made in 1899, and promoted Bryant & May, having the appropriate title of *Match Appeal*. Melbourne Cooper was an imaginative artist, a technician, and a true pioneer of three-dimensional puppetry.

James Stuart Blackton was another animator who made many experiments with the new medium, greatly advancing techniques for special effects through his innovations. Blackton, originally from Britain, settled in the USA and had an immense influence over the acceptance of animated films with general audiences. The title of his first film was *The Thief on the Roof*, released in November 1897. Like his other films which followed,

Blackton further bridged the gap between animated cartoon (made in stop-motion, frame-by-frame technique with artwork and a fixed camera) and live-action film (photographed in continuous motion with a mobile camera). History cites Blackton as one of the most important early practitioners of trick photography as well as of animation. With the collaboration of an expert cameraman called Albert Smith, he constructed a camera for trick photography called the Vitagraph (which was also to become the name of their film company). The camera first filmed the background to be used in a sequence; that 'exposure' was then wound back to the beginning and used to shoot the stop-motion part of the action. For this second exposure, the film was advanced frame by frame and the objects moved or adjusted according to the sequence. By controlling the amount of light allowed in, the second exposure was superimposed on top of the first. This system became widely adopted by other film-makers and animators in the years that followed.

Stuart Blackton's second contribution was the film *Humorous Phases of Funny Faces* (1906) which combined live, trick and animated techniques. The film starts with Blackton's own hand drawing the face of a man and then a woman. When the hand is removed, the cartoon man reacts to it by rolling his eyes; the cartoon woman then does the same. The man is given a cigar to smoke and a puff of smoke obliterates the woman's face. The smoke is real: it was superimposed over the drawings. Blackton's hand erases the faces and starts again with new tricks and new effects. It was a true animated cartoon with 'impossible' action where transitions of shapes and forms maintained the audience's interest. Blackton had taken a long time to make the film: he drew over 3000 drawings and exposed them several times to achieve the desired effects.

Blackton and Smith then made a film called *The Haunted Hotel*, which became a big hit after its release in March 1907 and resulted in prosperity for both its creators. For those early audiences, its simple cinematic tricks, such as a 'ghost' appearing and disappearing, objects moving on their own, tables being set by an invisible person and wine pouring itself into a glass, were totally magical images. The spectators were mystified as to how they were achieved but delighted nonetheless with the new form of entertainment. The French were quick to import *The Haunted Hotel* and it was shown in a large Parisian cinema (with a capacity of 5000) in Châtelet during July 1907.

At that time a popular formula was to present the performance live, with the artist producing speedily-drawn sketches onto a blackboard. The hall was then darkened and the characters apparently 'brought to life' when the film was projected onto a screen, this being the essence of the performance. This method of stage to screen is reputed to have originally come from Britain, introduced by a London newspaper cartoonist called Tom Merry, who sketched a portrait of Kaiser Wilhelm in this way in 1895. A sense of showmanship was needed in order to convince the audience.

It is possible that Emile Cohl, one of the first actual animated cartoonists, had seen Blackton's *Humorous Phases* in Paris and been strongly influenced by its 'magic'. It was easier, at that time, to distribute films imported from other countries and the Gaumont Studio's distribution department became the agents for Vitagraph Films, acquiring the rights of many of Blackton's films. Emile Cohl worked in the Gaumont Studios and would have had many opportunities to study the early American films using trick photography.

Cohl, who was born in 1857, was already middle-aged when he started his career as a cartoonist and developed a 'light-box' as an aid to the exact matching of animated drawings. He had a sense of cartoon timing which few of his predecessors possessed and a drawing skill way ahead of his contemporaries. His simple matchstick figures had a sophistication which his colleagues working for the newspapers could never even hope to achieve. By drawing eight individual figures for each second of film (at that time projected at sixteen frames per second), he achieved an unprecedented fluidity of movement, setting a standard which still exists today. Cohl followed the established convention of using either black lines against a white background or white lines against a black background, and both the narratives and the simple visual treatments were extremely easy to follow. However, Cohl became increasingly interested in exploring the subconscious through nightmares and hallucinations, rather than merely telling a story, and as such, many of his films seem incoherent. Nevertheless, those dealing with more ordinary human situations, such as *Un Drame Chez les Fantoches* (1908), contained a great deal of charm and subtle humour, telling the story of a typically French 'eternal triangle'. Cohl had a true instinct and a gift for his work: his timing was perfect and the gestures of his figures elegant. Even now, few have the facility for creating so much character animation within such a short time and with so much economy in the outline of the characters.

This neglected founder of the French animation industry died in abject poverty in 1938. His work, however, remains as a tribute to his artistry and skill, and in many ways marks the transition of animation from an offshoot of cinematography to an art form in its own right.

Above: Emile Cohl's classic matchstick figures in the film *Un Drame Chez les Fantoches* (1908)

FROM SCIENCE TO ART

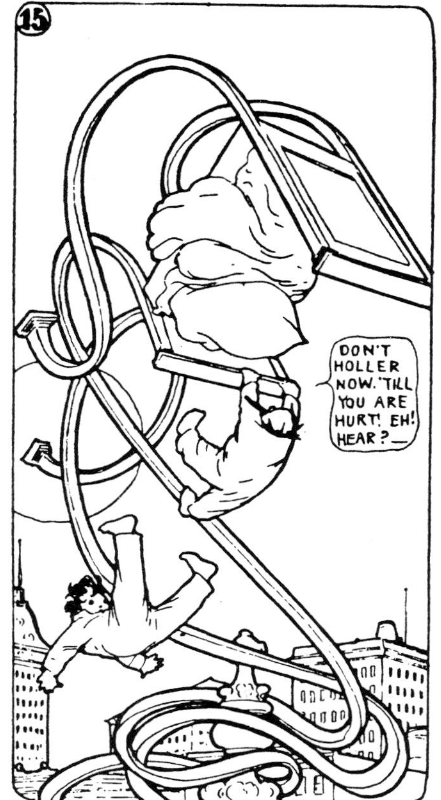

Above: two frames from Winsor McCay's *Little Nemo in Slumberland* (1911); right: McCay's Gertie the Dinosaur (1914), the first of many lovable cartoon creatures

During the first two decades of the twentieth century, animation developed from the mysterious realms of magic and wonderment into a form of entertainment which audiences accepted with delight. During this period, animators quickly learnt how to exploit the potential of the medium, creating memorable cartoon characters and discovering a flexibility of movement and timing which defied all the natural laws of physical possibilities.

It was an American, Winsor McCay, who achieved the earliest success in character creation by introducing the enchanting boy character Little Nemo and, later, Gertie the Dinosaur. *Little Nemo in Slumberland* originally appeared as a strip cartoon in the pages of the *New York Herald* in 1907, and Winsor McCay achieved enormous success when he decided to animate his drawings of Little Nemo and his friends in 1911. He used Nemo as the basis of his magician-style appearances on film and delighted the public with the beautiful, elaborately-drawn character. His first film with Little Nemo was advertised as the first attempt by an artist to draw pictures that could move. McCay's Gertie the Dinosaur first saw daylight in 1914: she was born as part of the stage act with McCay but gradually developed into a 'star' in her own right, outshining her creator. The contrast between Gertie's enormous bulk and her lovable, innocent nature soon won the audiences' hearts, establishing a link between comic strip, the vaudeville stage, and animated cartoons.

Winsor McCay was not only a showman, however, he was also a brilliant craftsman with a great talent for dramatic effects. A year after Gertie's début, he made what is often considered to be the first animated documentary film, *The Sinking of the Lusitania* (1915), giving stage-by-stage accounts of the dreadful event as described in the newspaper *The New York Telegram*. It is a highly dramatic, black and white film of the most complex nature: the scale is enormous and as the ship slowly sinks into the ocean, thousands of tiny human figures descend into the water and disappear beneath the waves. When I saw it for the first time I was very moved and afterwards marvelled at his courage in attempting to depict such a monumental and tragic event. I also learnt that McCay had produced 25,000 individual drawings, which was not only a physical achievement in his pre-computer times but comprised an historical document of a tragedy which happened in minutes without any visual record whatsoever.

It was around this period that the separate developments of American and European animation became apparent. In the USA, following the success of Stuart Blackton and Winsor McCay, studios popped up everywhere, as did animation personalities and their cartoon characters. Innovators such as John Randolph Bray and Raoul Barre were already established by 1915, for instance, and Hearst International started adapting comic strips into animated cartoons in 1916, producing *Krazy Kat*, *The Katzenjammer Kids* and *Little Jimmy*, among others.

In 1919, Felix the Cat was created in the studios of Pat Sullivan by Otto Messmer, and was produced under the title *Feline Follies*. Felix the Cat achieved a level of popularity comparable to the Disney characters which followed later, and was said to appeal especially to the more intellectual members of the audiences. The Felix films contained a huge number of visual gags which played upon the basic genre of the animated medium itself. When Felix used a question mark as a fishing hook and caught a fish, the animator was seen to be commenting on a functional metamorphosis which was only possible with animation. There were visual puns to delight the audience in practically every ten seconds of the film: examples of such inventive visual transformation were sustained throughout the production of the Felix 'shorts'.

Above: Max Fleischer's Koko the Clown in *Out of the Inkwell* was a brilliant comment on the nature of the animator's craft; above right: Betty Boop (1932) also from the Fleischer stable

Right: Victor Bergdahl's *The Adventures of Kapten Grogg* (1916); below: Felix the Cat (1919), creation of Otto Messmer

At around the same time, Max Fleischer's *Out of the Inkwell* series was developed along similar lines, with the added interest of a combination of live-action and animated film. Koko the Clown leapt into animated life out of an inkwell, assuming his existence from a blob of black ink.

Many of the 'big names' of animation were learning their trade at this time – Max and Dave Fleischer, Paul Terry, Walter Lantz and many others. Later, in the twenties and thirties, immortal characters such as Popeye and Woody Woodpecker emerged, still immensely popular with children and adults today.

In that period between the First and Second World Wars, cartoon animation in the USA had become both an enjoyable occupation for young artists and a favourite form of entertainment for the public, especially for the younger age group. Appealing to the older audiences, however, was Betty Boop, a character which had been developed by many young designers and groomed for years before she emerged in 1932 as a sex symbol, tailored to the image of Hollywood stars. Some critics actually found Betty more appealing than most live stars, presumably responding to the fact that, in developing a cartoon star, one only needs to emphasise the basic essence of a character. In the case of Betty, her delicate gestures, her oversized eyes and her innocence had a vulnerability and an ethereal quality which was inevitably lacking in most actresses.

In Europe, meanwhile, the scene for animators had been very different. Apart from occasional bursts of activity, little happened in the early days to develop animation into an industry as such. The USA, it seemed, had won the international race to define and shape the new medium.

For instance, some early Scandinavian films have been documented by film historian Torsten Jungstedt in Stockholm, which is where Victor Bergdahl (a local animator) came up with the series *The Adventures of Kapten Grogg*. Bergdahl's career resembled that of Winsor McCay: he was also a strip cartoonist turned animator and stage performer, making his sketches 'come to life'. He started making films in 1915 with a nine-minute film entitled *Trolldrycken*, probably the first animated cartoon about the effects of alcohol. He followed this up with a series of nineteen episodes based on Kapten Grogg's experiences around the world. Considering the

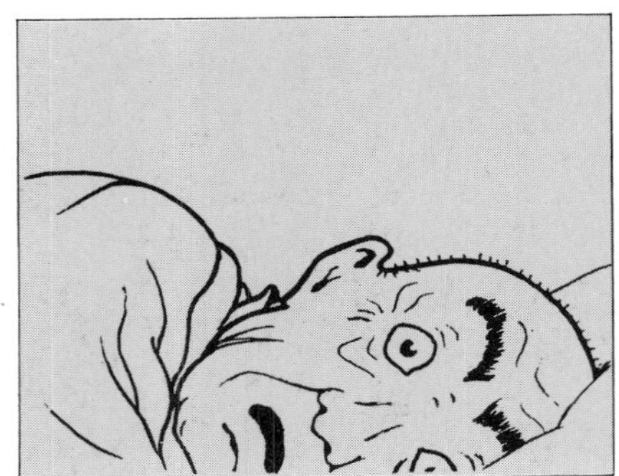

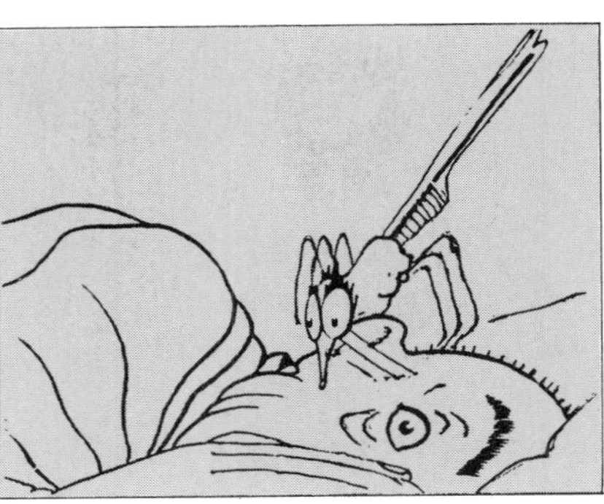

Above left and far left: *How a Mosquito Operates* (1910) by Winsor McCay; above: Victor Bergdahl's *The Demon Drink* (1915), clearly showing McCay's influence

circumstances and the small local market, these films were surprisingly well produced and enjoyed a great deal of public support. Victor Bergdahl's achievement inspired other cartoonists of that period, such as Paul Myren, M. R. Lijeqvist and Emil Aberq. Unfortunately, this was a short summer in Sweden lasting only a few years, tailing off around the start of the 1920s.

One of the problems for animators outside the USA may have been the fact that the impact of the imported American cartoons overshadowed the local productions which proved to be simply too expensive. Social changes in the USSR, for instance, stimulated their live-action film industry to become one of the leading lights of motion pictures, but conditions were not favourable for animation and that part of their film industry did not get started until the mid-twenties. It was then that it began to develop successfully, through the work of Alexander Buschkin, Alexander Ivanov, the Brumberg Sisters (Valentina and Sinaida) and Ivanov-Vano. The Brumbergs' first film, *China on Fire*, was made in 1925 and was followed by the production of at least one film a year, a formula which continues to this day. Russian animators soon discovered that the nation's wealth of fables, fairy-tales and traditional puppet theatre was an excellent source of material on which to base their work, primarily for children's entertainment.

Most of Europe during the post-war period of the 1920s did more thinking than doing. In general, film-makers were concerned with reshaping the way cinema was developing, and wanted to introduce new ideas based more on aesthetic concepts than technical ones. The sweeping influence of the abstract art movement; the separation of realist and impressionist cinema; the discovery of montage; the uses of superimposition and dissolves and the trend towards non-symmetrical composition all had an immense influence on the visual arts, including the production of animated films. This movement was motivated by the philosophy of the Bauhaus Design Institute, which set out to reform and unify the artistic disciplines of design, architecture, theatre and film. Out of this movement arose the non-figurative, abstract cartoon. In the forefront of the movement were artists like Viking Eggeling, Oscar Fischinger, Hans Richter, Walter Ruttman, Fernand Léger, Marcel Duchamp, Francis Picabia and Lászlo Moholy-Nagy, all of whom were concerned with motion dynamics.

Right: one of the woodcuts from *L'Idée* (1932) by Berthold Bartosch

The invention of a synchronised soundtrack also introduced a noticeable distinction between the ways in which European and American animation developed. In the USA, sound was primarily regarded as an ideal opportunity for improving characterisation. (One only has to imagine Donald Duck without his impatient quack to appreciate how much this element adds to a character's impact.) In Europe, however, sound was largely regarded as the exciting raw material for experimentation. The relationship between music, moving images and sound effects was explored to the full. Experimental animation came into focus with Oscar Fischinger's *Brahms' Hungarian Dances* (1931), utilising abstract mobile patterns in close synchronisation with the specific character of the music. In Paris, the Hungarian émigré, artist Berthold Bartosch, created *L'Idée* (1932), a film utilising a specially-written musical score by Honegger, the Swiss composer. It was an extremely accomplished animation of his etchings and woodcuts, telling the story of his flight to freedom; it opened to critical acclaim and was highly successful.

While the artistic possibilities of animation were being explored in Europe, however, an entirely different 'movement' was emerging in the USA. Out of the early experiments in characterisation and technique emerged the blossoming of what is now known as The Golden Age of American Cartoons.

It was a period which was noticeably free from cultural or intellectual pretensions: there was little brain power behind it, no philosophy, no

Right: an enduring pair, Mickey and Minnie Mouse; below: Walt Disney in 1939, at the piano with a few of his characters; opposite page, below: the manic Donald Duck in *Symphony Hour* (1942)

science, no academics. It was characterised by an enormous upsurge in the desire for fun and the need to develop one's inventive capacity for visual excitement. The period began in the early thirties.

Undoubtedly the most popular animation studio which began work at around this time was, of course, Walt Disney's. The spectacular rise of the Disney Studio into an internationally renowned centre of popular cartoon animation meant that it soon became the cradle of many young and talented artists.

Meanwhile, the name of Walt Disney, together with his vast range of characters led by the ubiquitous Mickey Mouse, became synonymous with popular, reliable family entertainment – indeed, with the medium of animation itself.

One of the continuing strengths of the Disney formula was the enormous amount of consideration which went into the planning of the storyboard. Disney invested far more time in this initial stage of production than did any other studio, and the value of this policy invariably paid off, as a huge percentage of the creative problems were solved before animation actually began.

From the late 1920s onwards, Disney's team of animators were in the vanguard of the popularisation of animated cartoons, the standard of their films becoming a yardstick by which other studios measured their own work. It was a tall order, however, and few characters ever became as internationally popular as Disney's Mickey Mouse, Minnie, Pluto, Goofy and Donald Duck.

The Disney Studio's output is discussed elsewhere (see pages 56–58), although for a detailed analysis one should turn to one of the many biographies which focus solely on Walt Disney and his studio. Something which is rarely mentioned, however, is the extent of the debt Disney owed to his Chief Animator, Ub Iwerks. Although Disney was an unparalleled story-teller and fabulist, Iwerks was a brilliant artist, animator and technician who eventually broke away from Disney in 1930, possibly due to what he felt was a lack of recognition. He returned, however, ten years later and once again became one of the most ingenious collaborators of the Studio. Indeed, it was Iwerks who extended the 'multiplane' photographic technique first developed in 1937 for *The Old Mill* and used it in *Fantasia* (1940), producing three-dimensional backgrounds for the first time in animated films.

The aims of the Studio inevitably changed after their establishment as the foremost proponents of the art. After the initial period of exploration and expansion, the once ambitious and challenging outlook became somewhat stagnant, with the emphasis increasingly falling on a cute-but-realistic style which was instantly accessible to popular audiences. By the early 1950s, this resulted in several internal rebellions amongst the artists, notably John Hubley who left to form the influential United Productions of America (see page 60).

The other side of the coin in the harsh competition with Disney was that, thanks to him, the other studios also prospered in the newly expanded market for animated cartoons. The Van Beuren Studio was founded in 1930, producing *Tom and Jerry* in 1937 and employing a number of highly-talented young animators such as Bill Littlejohn, Joseph Barbera and Jack Zander. After Van Beuren in 1930 came the Warner Studio in 1934, riding on the wave of public thirst for comedy, and under Leon Schlesinger produced the *Merrie Melodies*, *Looney Tunes*, *Porky and Beans*, *Daffy Duck* and *Bugs Bunny* series, with the artistry of Chuck Jones, Tex Avery, Bob Clampett and Abe Levitov.

By this time, animation had become a real profession, but the meaning of this goes much deeper than has been realised, even to this day. Dedication to the unique medium of animation has become an attitude, even an addiction to many of its practitioners, many of whom seem to have split personalities. They often appear unassuming, even meek from the exterior, but as soon as they grab their pencils they take on the aspects of mini-Gods, shaping and creating characters and scenarios out of their own imaginations. They know how to manipulate their drawing skill, how to make one character confront another and how to bring inanimate objects to life. A classic case in point is Max Fleischer's clown Koko, whose on-screen metamorphosis from a blob of ink into a clown makes a vivid and entertaining statement about the nature of animation. An act of this nature could only take place on the drawing board of an animator: the essence of the animator's skill is his or her power of manipulation.

Below and right: Elmer Fudd and Bugs Bunny, from the Warner Studio of the thirties

A legendary figure among animators is Tex Avery, who started working with Walter Lantz in the early 1930s writing stories and gags. He progressed to directing and animating Warner Brothers cartoons, developing such classic characters as Porky Pig, Daffy Duck and, with the young Chuck Jones, Bugs Bunny. Avery's skill has now been recognised by a new generation of enthusiasts who have rediscovered the value of the humorous absurdities and visual invention of American cartoons of that period. Avery was another example of a modest person whose exterior hid his power and daring behind the pencil. He knew how to exaggerate action successfully and he consistently over-stepped the limit, taking calculated risks which always paid off. He stretched his characters, he squeezed them, he made them behave outrageously and had effectively revolutionised animation by the middle of the 1950s. With his often violent gags and fast pace he kept his audience at a high tension, never letting them relax. His subjects, which were usually concerned with either survival, status or sex, always established immediate audience identification and interest.

Psychologically, the audience became virtually addicted to the comic relief of watching cartoon characters perform or survive feats which they themselves could not have enacted. This vicariousness as a function of animation was utilised further in the confrontations between characters, especially when a vulnerable one triumphed over a bully. Audiences also discovered that the freedom of animation removed both pain and guilt: a character could hurt or be hurt without emotional or physical comeback.

The Tex Avery, Chuck Jones and Bob Clampett cartoons achieved world-wide success, and it was quite useless for European animators to try to copy them. They had an American flavour, combining childlike visual invention, good clean fun, slapstick humour and draughtsmanship of the highest order. Few attempted to criticise human failings, social conditions or psychological complexities: the problems of the world were left to politicians and writers. These films were simple to follow and were uncomplicated in their form and content: if there was any moralism behind the story-lines, the general message was that, quite simply, good must on all account win over bad. The Big Bad Wolf must be outwitted and punished. Even before the Second World War, however, it appears that some of the steam ran out of the American cartoon industry. Repetitions were frequent and it is possible that the public became too accustomed to the gag cartoon format.

Many talented cartoonists turned their hand to help the war effort with propaganda films, such as Bob Clampett, Tex Avery and the young Friz Freleng. The Disney Studio, with its reduced personnel, concentrated on doing instructional films for the Navy and propaganda films for the Government. The success of the operation was mixed. The restrictions of a tight brief, the discipline of a narrow propaganda message and the limitations of a low budget were not easy conditions for animators accustomed to open-ended comedy shorts. However, considering the circumstances, the

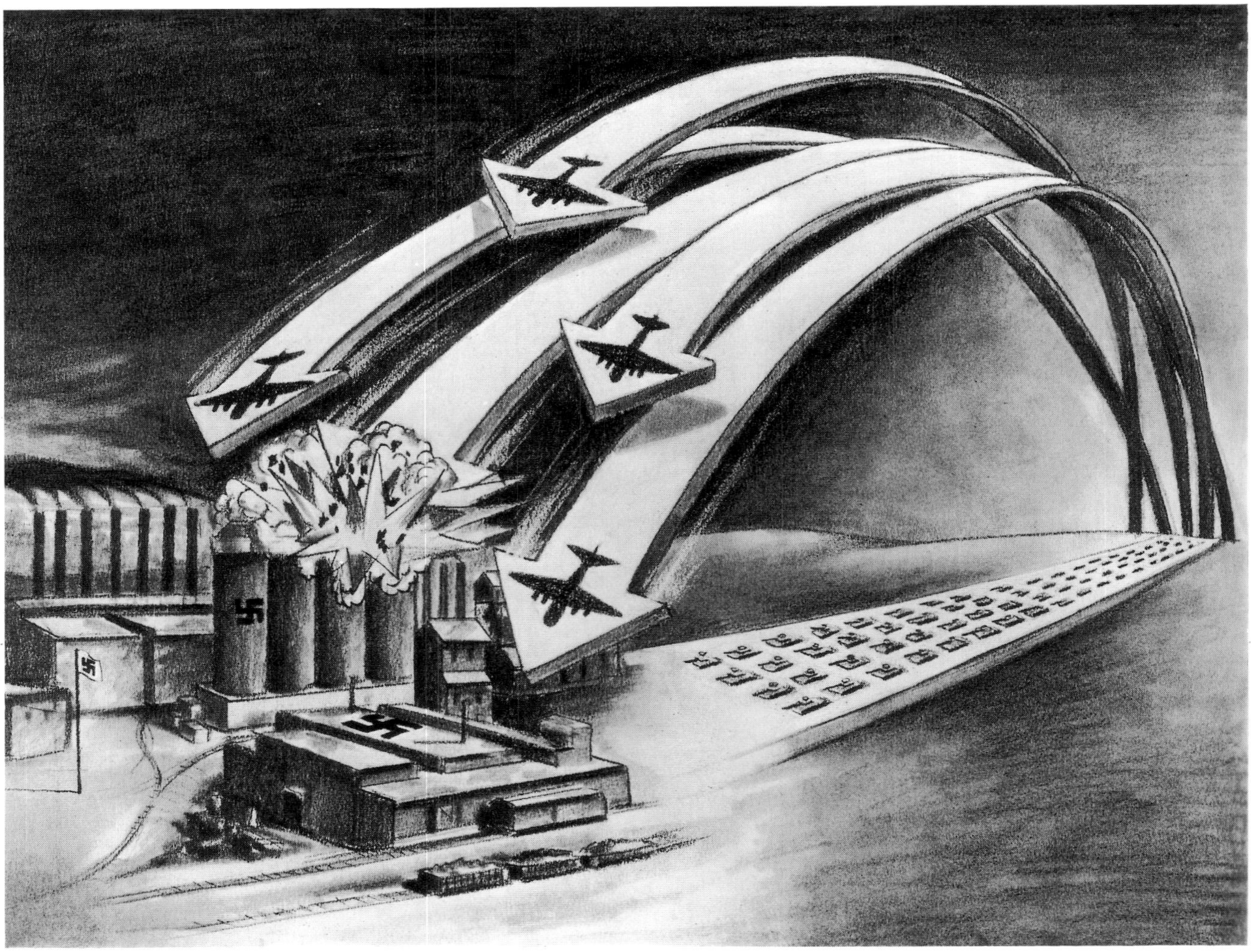

Disney Studio did very well with the long film *Victory Through Air Power* which successfully boosted American morale.

In Europe, especially in Britain, the medium of animation was beginning to pick up. Our new studio, Halas and Batchelor (see page 82), was recruited by the Ministry of Information to concentrate on aspects of the war effort such as saving scrap metal for guns – *Dustbin Parade* (1941), growing vegetables – *Digging for Victory* (1941), and keeping a lookout for spies – *Abu's Harvest* (1943). The small unit made over seventy films for the Ministry, all of which were widely distributed in cinemas throughout the country. Because of this, when the war was over there was quite a scramble for our services, which were needed to explain to the public the various changes and reforms in the social structure, through the accessible medium of animation. These films, with a 'man in the street' character called Charley, had a strong adult appeal, but would not be described as comedy films. They appealed to the British public's common sense, using a well-reasoned argument instead of humour to win favour and understanding. Later, this format was widely adopted by the rest of the industry. It was to some extent due to this work of our unit that the application of animation was able to broaden out and achieve new objectives. The medium began to be used for public relations, for the advertisement of major corporations and for education. Freed from the restrictions of having to tell a quick, dynamic, funny tale, there was time to develop a fresh-looking graphic style which was quickly taken up by other nations in western Europe.

Above: a scene from the Disney Studio's highly effective wartime film *Victory Through Air Power* (1943); below: a preliminary sketch for Halas and Batchelor's *Abu's Harvest* (1943)

THE DEVELOPMENT OF THE CARTOON FEATURE

Few people know – and unfortunately one must include some animators among them – how difficult it is to make a feature-length animated film. Unless one has the resources, the infinite patience, the technical understanding of the process, the experience and, most of all, the energy and determination, the project will not succeed. This was the reason why so many feature films were started and so few completed during the period prior to the Second World War.

It took quite some time, and many experiments, for animators to realise that it is not simply a matter of trying to string together a number of short films to make a long one. One has to construct a coherent, properly developed story, just as for a live-action film, in order to keep the attention of the audience. The lesson was eventually learnt, but unfortunately only through the failure of many studios.

Part of the difference between short and long animated films lies in the audience's response. The majority of short animated cartoons last between six and eight minutes, and a fast pace and lots of action is sufficient to maintain interest and amusement. With the longer features, however, it is crucial for the audience to become actually involved in the development of the narrative, if the eighty minutes of screen time is not to feel like an eternity.

Short animated cartoons can begin and end with a physical confrontation between two characters: Tom and Jerry or Sylvester and Tweety Pie are cases in point. Starting with a series of gags and a chase sequence with the roles reversed several times, the animator can keep an audience transfixed from beginning to end. The fact that the characters commit ostensibly damaging, sadistic acts during the inevitable long-drawn-out chase (which would not pass with even the most benevolent censor if they were committed in a live-action film) does not matter. At that level cartoon characters remain what they essentially are: drawn symbols devoid of human pain; figures of fun; capable of impossible deeds. This type of cartoon animation – and there are many other types – depends mainly on the appeal of action and movement.

In a feature-length production, these elements may well be present but audiences are easily bored by too much of them, especially if the action becomes repetitious. The cartoon feature requires a dramatic atmosphere, a story, and continuous development culminating in a climactic denouement. Live-action film can maintain interest through extended scenes of dialogue and acting: to maintain a visual identity is easier as the depiction of reality is within the scope of the live-action camera lens. The animator has to work very much harder to achieve the desired effect. Cartoon features are a special kind of medium, demanding a particular discipline and a totally different format. The most successful types have so far depended on the appeal of established legends and fantasy: the fairy-tales and folk-tales with which the public is already familiar and which they are delighted to see recreated in an entirely new form, seeing favourite characters come to life.

Below: like Tom and Jerry, Friz Freleng's Sylvester and Tweety Pie (1947) exemplified the short cartoon formula

Full-length animated films go back a surprisingly long way. In 1916 in Italy, Segundo de Chomón and Giovanni Pastrone made a number of animated films, among them a long, combined puppet and live-action film entitled *La Guerra E Il Sogno Di Momi*. We also now know that Quirino Cristiani, an Italian-born cartoonist, made a long feature called *El Apostol* in Argentina in 1917. The subject of this sixty-minute production was satirical, and the film contained some humorous looks at the political and social conduct of a President and his Ministers. (In 1981, more than half a century after the completion of *El Apostol*, Quirino Cristiani directed, produced and wrote another long film, *Peludopoles*, which was also a political satire, this time on President Irigoyen.)

Meanwhile, in Germany, out of the gloom and extreme poverty of the twenties came a remarkable experiment by an art student, Lotte Reiniger, using cut-out paper forms which she animated frame by frame under the camera, over a flat wooden board. She found that she could get better visual effects by using silhouette forms, which provided a more positive contrast for the tones of her figures. After several years of work with her primitive camera, she completed her feature film in 1926. It was called *The Adventures of Prince Achmed*, which, in the same year, opened in Paris at the Comédie des Champs-Elysées.

The production of the early French animated feature film *The King and the Bird* started during 1935 as a partnership between André Sarrut and Paul Grimault. They were without adequate funds, and had more ambition and enthusiasm than experience. The two men (the first a promoter, the latter a highly-talented artist) did not get on well and the many differences

Left: Lotte Reiniger's *The Adventures of Prince Achmed* (1926), one of the earliest animated feature films and made entirely with paper cut-outs

of opinion caused delays. Eventually the production was stopped and only renewed after the war. Again, it was not a success and had to be abandoned. However, with admirable courage and determination, Paul Grimault resumed the work in 1977, modernising both the artwork and the style of animation. He released his feature in 1979 to well-deserved acclaim, both from the critics and the public.

The intervention of Walt Disney and his team into the development of the animated feature film, however, took the medium to a new level of sophistication. In 1937, they released *Snow White and the Seven Dwarfs*, a film which also had far-reaching implications for the Disney Studio itself. By the mid-thirties, the Studio had developed the necessary facilities to tackle this, their most ambitious project yet. They had already achieved a considerable success with their series of shorts such as the *Silly Symphonies*; they had the artistic talents; they knew how to create a rounded cartoon personality; they had the intelligence to know the difference between the restrictions of real, live-action timing and the free manipulation of cartoon timing; they had enough money to see them through the production and they had the technical resources for photography, sound recordings and editing. The result was that the Disney unit generated so much confidence in this first feature-length production that it became the most significant step forward in the life of that already distinguished studio.

Snow White was made in the Studio when Disney had already established an experienced production system. It was mainly a question of, firstly, building on its foundations by attracting new, enthusiastic young artists to enlarge the existing studio, and secondly, accomplishing the task within a tight, well-organised production unit. The film took three years to complete with a large personnel of artists, technicians and production staff, all of whom had a pioneering dedication to be involved in the creation of the first 'smash-hit' animated feature film.

All of the previous full-length animated films had been produced in black and white and had inevitably made little impact with general audiences, as the medium was still in the early stages of development. In contrast, Disney's *Snow White* benefited from the use of colour, a sophisticated sound treatment with excellent music, voices full of character and a highly professional skill in story-telling. Each animated figure was carefully developed as visual synonym for their basic character and was 'groomed' for their part in the film. It has been claimed that, as a film for children, the character development was sometimes too perfect, too sharp and too convincing. Since the technique of animation necessitates a certain amount of overemphasis, many characters became very frightening for the young audience. The story goes that when *Snow White* was first presented at the Radio City Music Hall, the transformation of the Queen into the Witch/pedlar woman scared the children so much that many of the velvet seats had to be replaced! In our television age, it is possible that today's young children have developed a greater degree of resistance to fear, but for the children of the thirties, the Witch was a fully developed villainess taking shape before their eyes and the effect of her power, through skilful animation, made her a formidable character.

Animators often maintain that a certain degree of exaggeration is essential in order to engage audience participation, their hate, sympathy and overall concern. The medium of animation seemed problematic at that time, however, with its tendency to sensationalise and with its initial difficulties in finding a mid-way between extremes. The Disney Studio quickly learnt how to exploit this capacity, and during many of the subsequent feature productions were able to utilise frightening situations to their full extent, sweetening the story just enough to avoid an adverse effect on children and adolescents. The exploitation of the young puppet in *Pinocchio* (1940), the fear of flying in *Dumbo* (1941), and the fear of abandonment and losing one's mother in *Bambi* (1942), for instance, were all charged with both emotional dynamite and great doses of sentimentality in their final conclusions. The tension, therefore, was successfully resolved.

Snow White certainly deserved the world-wide attention and acclaim it received, which was quickly capitalised upon by the Disney films which followed. Released in the same year as *Pinocchio*, but very different in theme and treatment, was the experimental *Fantasia*, an ambitious visualisation of several musical compositions, such as Stravinsky's *Rite of Spring* and Tchaikovsky's *Nutcracker Suite*. This was a project which showed clear evidence of Disney's awareness of the European experiments being conducted at that time with aural and visual coordination and the use of abstract forms (see page 25).

The public, meanwhile, by the sheer force of Disney's promotion of *Snow White* and the almost annual impact of the subsequent films, assumed that Disney was the first animator ever to break the barrier between short and long animated films.

Nevertheless, the pattern was set by Disney and others quickly followed it, such as the Fleischer Brothers with two productions: *Gulliver's Travels* (1939) made in their studio in Maine, and *Mr Bug Goes to Town* (1940). While the fluidity of animation and the technical execution was of a high standard, the skill in story-telling fell very short, lagging behind the Disney Studio's attention to detail and character building.

At Halas and Batchelor in the early fifties, we felt that *Animal Farm* was another example of pioneering exploration, from the point of view of its content and its production, since it was destined to be the first ever animated feature film to be made in Britain. George Orwell's brilliant and subtle tale about an animal revolution is not exactly a light-hearted children's comedy. It is a serious, political satire about the exploitation of a group of workers who eventually take possession of their own community, only to discover that they are then just as ill-treated by a minority within their own ranks. The medium of animation had never tackled such an intellectual subject before and the task was to take the animated film towards a new level of

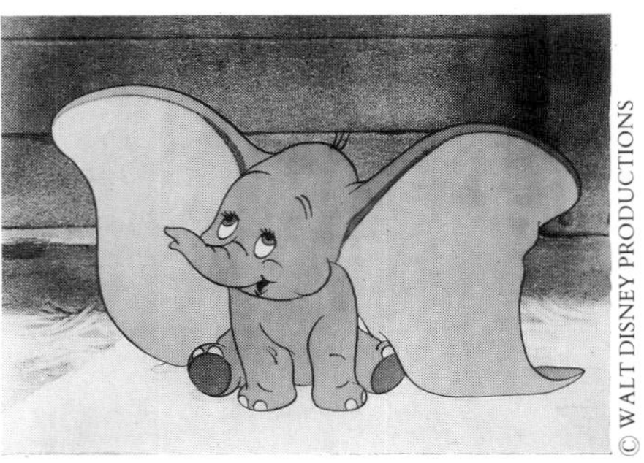

Above: Walt Disney's *Dumbo* (1941). The Disney Studio of the early 1940s displayed unparalleled talent for strong narratives and emotional manipulation

Above: the loyal carthorse, Boxer, in *Animal Farm* (1954) by Halas and Batchelor; below right: *The Point* (1970) by Fred Wolf and Chuck Swenson

maturity and acceptability. The technical conception was just as complex as the artistic. Up to that point, the Halas and Batchelor studio employed less than twenty staff working on sponsored industrial and propaganda films, and few could be spared to join the production of a feature film. The task was to establish a crash course for young animators; to teach, guide and produce as one went along. Within a year we had to construct a competent, well-administered, creative studio of seventy personnel, and to maintain a constant output. This eventually amounted to a thousand individual drawings and painted sheets of celluloid, which went to make up a feature film of just over seventy minutes long. The production commenced in April 1951 and was completed in November 1954.

Today, with modern facilities and technology, much time could be saved in production, especially with labour-saving apparatus for the 'in-between shots' and computer-driven photographic cameras. Machines, however, are no use without ideas and artistic inspiration, especially in the complex production of feature-length films.

There is a clear guideline for the genre of animation, which applies more to features than to short films, and it is a comparatively simple one. If a story or a subject can be adequately and expressively filmed with live-action, it should not be animated. To some extent, animation must begin where reality ends, and its best sources are stories from out of this world, the world of fantasy and imagination. If the story construction is skilful and the subject is recognisable and sympathetic, it will have a universal appeal. It should be said, however, that the animated feature film remains a

Above: Ralph Bakshi's *American Pop* (1981)

very difficult format and its potential is still to be explored. At the time of writing, notable and innovative feature-length productions have so far reached a dozen, and altogether, less than 500 animated feature films have been produced world-wide since the first long films were made in Italy and Argentina over half a century ago. The ability and resources required to produce an animated feature film are extremely rare and the problems involved are many and varied. Little of the initial promise of the animated feature has really been fulfilled up to the present time and it is to be hoped that, with the introduction of further and more sophisticated technology, a new wave of productions will be forthcoming, realising the enormous potential inherent in the medium.

PART TWO

THE INTERNATIONAL PANORAMA

THE COUNTRIES

Alongside the artistic development of the animated cartoon between the First and Second World Wars were its technical advances, its struggles for recognition – or at least economic survival – and its growing popularity with adolescent audiences in the USA. These aspects were mirrored in practically every nation which already had a film industry. Although animated films did become universally accessible (in the sense that, to a large extent, dialogue was optional as their format was primarily visual), their actual production still had to take place in the major cities: the urban areas where there was both demand for it and vital facilities such as drawing and editing equipment and laboratories for developing and printing film. New studios grew up in London, Moscow, Montreal, Rome, Paris and in most other Western capital cities. Each one of them had to establish themselves from the start with available resources, and had to survive with little reference to studios in other lands. Where they received state subsidies, in the USSR and the other eastern European nations for instance, the problem of survival was not so acute; in other countries, such as Britain, France and Italy, animation studios had to survive through commissions of various kinds, such as those for advertising films and orders from industry and governments for educational and informational films. Some nations, like Canada, were luckier than others.

What follows is a brief look at several of the countries where animation has become a part of the mainstream culture, to a greater or lesser degree. Later in this chapter there is a section on some masters of the art and their individual contributions to the animation industries of the world.

Above: one of Fritz's incarnations in *The Nine Lives of Fritz the Cat* (1974) by Steve Krantz and Robert Taylor (a follow-up to Ralph Bakshi's original *Fritz the Cat* in 1971); below: *Puff the Magic Dragon* (1978) by Fred Wolf and Chuck Swenson

USA

As we have seen in the previous chapter, much of animation's development as a medium took place in the USA: indeed, its sophistication as a major form of entertainment for children was largely the work of one American studio, that of Walt Disney (see page 56). Since then, numerous animators have added to the wealth of American animation: Chuck Jones, John and Faith Hubley and Barrie Nelson (see pages 59, 60 and 62) to name only a very few.

During the last couple of decades, however, animation in the USA has been under the stranglehold of the demands of the television market. The hugely profitable area of television depends largely upon mass production working methods which, unfortunately, usually produce animated films to match. There have been, however, some brave attempts at breaking out of this mould, producing some high points of both inspired and popular animation. Some well-known examples are *Puff the Magic Dragon* (1978) and *The Point* in the early seventies, both by Fred Wolf and Chuck Swenson:

Above: Jules Engel's *Train Landscape* (1977); below: J. Borenstein's *Traveller's Palm* (1976)

they were extremely well designed and executed, and acclaimed as exciting television specials. The satirical *Fritz the Cat* (1971) was an enterprising and highly imaginative cartoon feature by Ralph Bakshi.

One of the most impressive contributions, perhaps, came from Jules Engel, a former artist with United Productions of America (UPA), who made some outstanding films drawing heavily on contemporary art. In *Accident* (1974), *Wet Paint* (1976) and *Train Landscape* (1977), abstract forms came alive, once again affirming the potential of non-figurative animated film. Engel is also the head of experimental animation at the California Institute of Arts, and many of his students are among the most promising new talents in the USA.

There is a strong feeling amongst many young American animators that the time has come to abandon the traditional image of character animation. Many of the new generation are not interested in maintaining the school established by such Disney masters as Frank Thomas, Ollie Johnston, Art Babbitt and Grim Natwick. Today's ideal medium is thought by many to be the computer rather than the drawing board, and modern heroes include such pioneers as John Whitney Snr, who is one of the earliest experimenters in digital animation. Whitney began with *Film Exercise #1* (1943), and *Mozart Rondo* (1952), carrying on his work into the sixties with *Motion Graphics* (1967) and *Permutations* (1968), and into the seventies with *Matrix I* (1971). The new values in animation are inventiveness through graphics and vivid pictorialism: for better or worse many animators of this new generation do not regard realistic movement and sharp characterisation as important areas in which to invest talent and energy. The development of this more contemporary type of animation (of which many of the major innovators are either from, or are working in, the USA) is discussed in Part Three.

CANADA

Little was achieved in the field of Canadian animation until the establishment of the National Film Board of Canada in 1939, by the legendary Scotsman, John Grierson. The country was too close to the USA to develop its own industry, and only Briant Fryer succeeded in contributing to the medium with his animated shadow puppet theatre. Grierson was already a top film-maker with an international reputation, producing socially-orientated documentaries in Britain. In laying the foundations of NFBC he gave Canada a major transplant of talent: he invited his collaborators from Britain in both sectors – live action and animation. Many took up his offer, including Norman McLaren (see page 64). Originality was actively encouraged, and adherence to the ideal of close team-work prevented the growing animation unit from becoming an American-style mass-production studio. Instead, the individual artists retained a sense of creative freedom: this policy was adopted from the start and still prevails.

As time developed, the list of distinguished productions grew. Norman McLaren was breaking new ground in animation techniques, and winning prizes (including Oscars) for his brilliant experimental films.

The overall objective was to project Canada both to the Canadians and to people abroad. With the ideal medium of animation, which can so easily transcend language barriers, this was felt to have been achieved almost instantly. Later, the animation units split into English and French sectors, and again attracted talents like a magnet. Gerry Potterton, Derek Lamb, Mike Mills and Les Drew from London; Kaj Pindal from Denmark, Alexandre Alexeieff and Claire Parker (see page 96) from France, Paul Driessen (see page 112) and Co Hoedeman from Holland, Caroline Leaf (see page 63) and Lynn Smith from the USA, Peter Foldes from France, Ishu Patel (see page 68) from India and Zlatko Grgic from Yugoslavia. Today, this magnificent interchange of talent continues to the obvious benefit of all concerned.

Meanwhile, as the National Film Board proceeded with their enlightened policy, the Canadian Broadcasting Corporation in Montreal also started their animation unit, headed by the graphic designer Hubert Tison. The objective of the unit was primarily to serve the need for television programme titles, announcements and inserts. Moreover, the French sector of CBC Radio Canada had the foresight to test the skill of their graphic design staff in animated graphics and produced a number of astonishingly good short films for children such as *Everything for Nothing* (1978) by Frédéric Back (see page 66), *The Tortoise and the Hare* (1979) by Graeme Ross and *Trapeze* (1982) by Alberto Mino Bonan.

Nowadays, most of the new generation of talented Canadian animators come through the Sheridan College animation school in Toronto. Some become notable for their excellent productions even before they reach the professional market, such as Jon Minnis with his film *Charade*, which won an Oscar in 1985.

JAPAN

Although the Japanese have a long tradition of design which goes back several thousand years, it was a while before animation and film graphics became established art forms in Japan. Before the Second World War there were only a few artists interested in the medium and most of them, such as Ofuji, worked in three-dimensional puppetry with primitive cameras.

The situation today is very different. Japan has become the top nation in the production of commercial television animation for children and there

Left: Lynn Smith's *The Sound Collector* (1982); below left: Alberto Mino Bonan's *Trapeze* (1982); right: Sumio Gotoda's *A Mini Symphony*; below: Shinichi Suzuki's *A Point* (1972)

are around 25,000 individuals engaged in the Japanese animation industry, working mainly in big studios. These studios have to maintain a continuous output in order to satisfy the seemingly unlimited demand for children's entertainment on television, and to produce feature films for the cinemas. In this climate of large studios and mass-production methods, individual artists have to struggle for survival just as they do in western Europe. In contrast to the animators of the custom-made television films and commercials, the independent film designers have practically no outlet for their work.

It wasn't until the highly individual artist, Yoji Kuri, began work that the world was aware that innovative and distinguished film graphics existed at all in Japan. Until the early sixties, most Japanese animated films resembled pale imitations of the work of Hollywood animators, without the humour. The abstract linear designs of Yoji Kuri contained all the elements of modern graphics and dry wit although executed in typically Japanese style. Interestingly, Kuri's films were first released in the West, and it was not until they had met with relative success there that they were shown in Japan itself.

Since then, Renzo Kinoshita (see page 71) has produced some remarkable cartoon films and Kihachiro Kawamoto (see page 69) has taken three-dimensional puppet animation a step further by producing distinctive films based on traditional Japanese fairy-tales. Osamu Tezuka (see page 73) has specialised in feature-length animated films in Mushi Productions, and in spite of his popular figurative approach has maintained a unique graphic style, mainly through his background design.

Among the new generation of film-makers, Masaki Fujihata and Ko Nakajima's work probably spans the widest range of experimentation, particularly in subject matter. Fujihata's background includes acting, theatre design, advertising and publishing, and he brings much of this experience into his work while still managing to retain a strong sense of his personality in the designs.

Japanese animation can at last claim to be developing a unique style in a variety of subject areas. This, however, is surely only the beginning: the climate is right for expansion and the national tradition of design combined with achievements in high technology should provide the means to explore this exciting medium further.

Above: Anson Dyer's character, Sam, created in 1934; below: two frames from a commercial for Club Mediterranée by Ian Moo Young, *Francs for the Memory*; bottom: Ian Moo Young's commercial for Rice Krispies, *Breakfast Sounds*

GREAT BRITAIN

The first signs of the establishment of a British tradition in animation emerged in the twenties with the work of Anson Dyer. He began work during the First World War, a time when many film cartoonists had just learnt the trade by assisting in the nation's war efforts. Dyer was the first British animator to form a professional studio and properly divide the work into different departments. From being not only the animator but the designer, scriptwriter and camera operator too, Dyer delegated these functions in 1924 to a team of specialists, and a continuous output began to pour from his studio. Dyer's best work was made in 1934: a series of films introducing a marvellous character called Sam. Unfortunately these films, although professional in technique, lacked the exuberance of high spirits and visual images of the American cartoons at the time. They appeared heavy and laboured in comparison and never really took off with the public. When this important personality died in 1952, the studio's entire personnel and resources were utilised in our production of *Animal Farm* at Halas and Batchelor (see page 82).

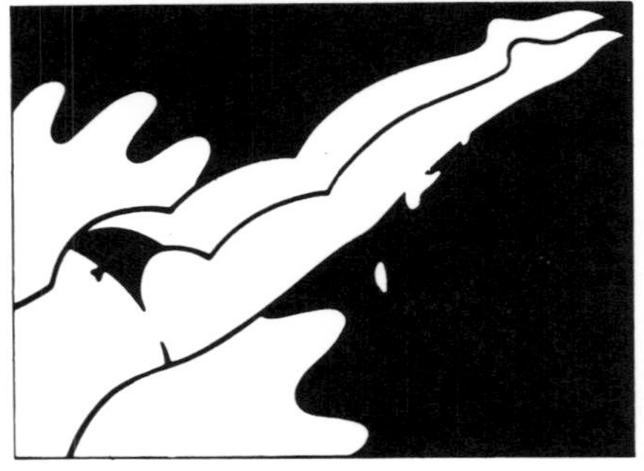

Possibly the most interesting event of the post-Second World War period for animators in Britain was in 1947 when the Rank Organisation 'imported' David Hand, a Hollywood animator from the Disney stable. It was hoped that Hand's visit would energise the British animation scene. He returned to the USA in 1951, however, having made little impact. Britain's animators, it was said, could not be forced to adopt American methods of mass-production.

Nevertheless, a big expansion did begin in the fifties. The W.M. Larkins Studio, where the young Geoff Dunbar began (see page 84), had considerable success in 1954 with a business film called *Enterprise* for ICI, which was a film made to show financial results in an amusing way. The advent of commercial television, moreover, had a dramatic effect on British animation. Studios sprang up like mushrooms.

In the forefront were Richard Taylor, Bob Godfrey (see page 79) with the Biographic Studio, and the two Tonys: Tony Wyatt and Tony Cattaneo. Later, many others followed, notably Phil Austin, Derek Hayes, the Canadian George Dunning (see page 80) and the outstanding Alison de Vere, whose film *Café Bar* (1975) established her as a major talent and whose *Mr Pascal* (1979) won several international awards.

It is interesting to note that more than half of the present studios in Britain were established in the early 1980s, and they quickly made a strong impact on the animation market; notable among them is Ian Moo Young's studio. They are able to maintain a freshness in their visual approach, an understanding about the necessity of original ideas and a flexibility in adapting their techniques to the specific requirements of an assignment.

Above: Count Pushkin Vodka in *Trans Siberian Express* (1974) by Rowland B. Wilson and Russell Hall; below: a still from Dianne Jackson's animated version of Raymond Briggs' *The Snowman* (1985)

Animation City has done some outstanding films, including *Sky Whales* (1983) and *The Victor* (1985). Cosgrove-Hall Productions in Manchester have been able to maintain a high standard of television cartoon series and are now expanding with new feature-length films for the cinema. Cucumber Studios in London have earned a reputation for their first-class graphic design and their understanding of new techniques and new processes.

Since the introduction of a local television service in Wales, a number of successful animation studios are operating there, such as Siriol and Fairwater Films. It is to their credit that they have expanded their operation to such an extent that Siriol's series, with their character SuperTed, now runs on the 'Disney Channel' in Hollywood.

Meanwhile, a promising new generation has emerged from the film and animation colleges in Britain. Jonathan Hodgson's *Nightclub* (1983), made while he was still at the Royal College of Art, stood up well amongst international productions at the Annecy Film Festival in 1983. Susan Young's excellent film *Carnival* (1985) was from the same college, and Alison Snowden's *Second Class Mail* (1985) was from the National Film & Television School at Beaconsfield. Iain McCall's *Christmas for Sale* from Liverpool Polytechnic won an award at the London Film Festival in 1984.

Britain today, with over a thousand artists in a rapidly growing industry, has become one of the leading nations in the world, where experiments, visual inventions, and progressive aesthetics and techniques are very much in the forefront. It is interesting to note that there are now twenty-seven British design colleges teaching the art of animation, and the quality of much of the students' work promises to maintain Britain's position as one of the leading nations in the world of animation.

YUGOSLAVIA

One of the most interesting flowerings of European animation has been in Yugoslavia, through the remarkable success of the Zagreb Animated Film Studio. Zagreb, a relatively small town, has had a flourishing animation studio since 1956, and has regularly produced prize-winning films ever since, so much so that its films have become identified as products of 'The Zagreb School of animation'.

Among the first to attract attention were Dušan Vukotić (see page 75), Vatroslav Mimica and Nikola Kostelac, whose films made an outstanding impact when they were first presented at the Cannes International Film Festival. The films contained new concepts in both content and form, and were entirely original in design.

Many others came along to boost the growing reputation of the studio: Borivoj Dovniković (see page 78) was a former strip cartoonist who made

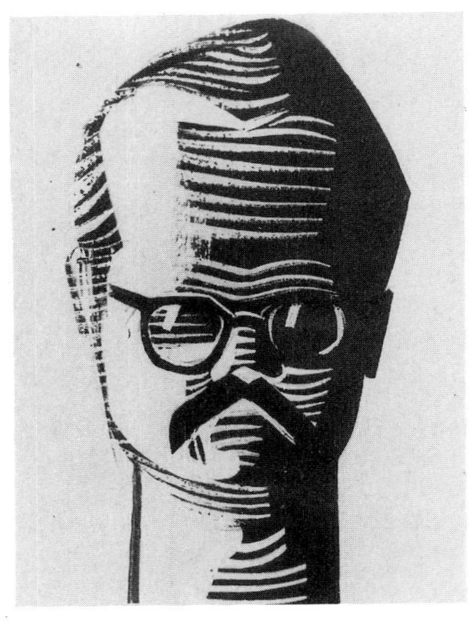

Above left: Vatroslav Mimica's *Režiser*; above: Zdenko Gasparovic's *Satiemania* (1978); below: Moholy-Nagy's experiment in abstract, animated shadows, *Light Space Modulator* (1923–1930)

many humorous animated cartoons, as was Nedeljko Dragic (see page 76), although the latter utilised a more dynamic style and a savage visual humour. Bourek was a painter who brought many surreal images to the screen; Ante Zaninovic contributed his dry, biting wit; and Zdenko Gasparovic, whose film *Satiemania* (1978) successfully bridged the gap between animation and the fine arts, also joined the studio.

Zagreb Animated Film Studio has succeeded in maintaining its record of outstanding productions for over thirty years. Few would deny that, apart from the medium of sculpture, Yugoslavian art has been represented world-wide by this single studio. Others opening up in Novigrad, Belgrade and Skopje have now added to the wealth of activity in Yugoslavian animation, and the established tradition of talent, individuality and professionalism will no doubt ensure that its reputation will continue.

HUNGARY

Between 1928 and 1933, Hungary was in the forefront of the development of abstract animation. Several of the Bauhaus teachers in Germany went on to open up colleges in Budapest, with the intention of furthering the aims of the Bauhaus design revolution. They were dedicated to finding new creative forms which expressed the functional simplicity they desired, eliminating all elements of visual elaboration and creating a new aesthetic order. The art of moving pictures was as much a part of the curriculum as architecture, graphics, stage design or photography.

During this period, while German experimentalists such as Fischinger and Richter (see page 24) were making their abstract animated films in Berlin, László Moholy-Nagy and Alexander Bortnyik in Budapest started to experiment with their own. I had the privilege of assisting both of them. Moholy-Nagy was nearer to the experimental art of photography with his elaborately patterned shadows of mobile metallic plates. He constructed an intricate mobile out of perforated aluminium discs, plastic, steel and glass plates, suspended on a frame. He then fitted the mobile into an electric circuit and controlled his multicoloured light sources as the construction turned round and round. The patterns produced an intricate display of

Above: Gyula Macskassy's *Duel* (1961); above right: Peter Szoboszlay's *Te! He!*; below: Josef Gemes' *Dalias Idök* (*Heroic Times*) (1985)

flickering lights and shadows which he then photographed: the effect on the screen was an unforgettable impression of abstract magic. Bortnyik had an entirely different idea about animation: as a graphic designer he was more interested in the figurative possibilities of the new art. Among his many experiments in animation, possibly the most interesting project was one which involved an animated film of Bortnyik's self-portrait coming to life and erasing itself. It took a year for the film to reach half-way and was never finished: he lost interest, as so many other easel painters and graphic artists have, being unused to the laborious process of animation.

Meanwhile, a brilliant college student named George Pal was making short advertising cartoons for local firms at the rate of one a day. The story, artwork, photography and laboratory processing for each film had to be done from morning to evening, so that it could be shown in the cinemas the following day. I was apprenticed to him for four years and gained invaluable experience from this high-speed work, as well as from Pal's fanatical attention to detail, his careful consideration of audience reaction, and his artistic instinct.

After the Second World War, Pal went on to Hollywood and became one of the pioneers of American science fiction films. For myself, I established an animation studio in collaboration with Gyula Macskassy in 1932: later, we were joined by the well-known caricaturist Felix Kassowitz, and we became the Colortron Studio. Our unit produced forty-two short films – both commercial and experimental – in four years.

Hungarian animation finally blossomed, however, when Pannonia Film was established in 1950. With restless energy and ardent dedication, the Studio's team soon produced a number of high-quality films, including *Duel*, directed by Gyula Macskassy for Unesco. A talented team of animators soon emerged, among them Marcell Jankovics and Attila Dargay (see pages 86 and 88), Sandor Reichenbuchler, Josef Nepp (see page 89) and Josef Gemes, who assisted in the direction of several feature films financed by American investors (such as *Hugo the Hippo*). The experience enabled Gemes to make *Dalias Idök (Heroic Times)* which won the Best Feature Film prize at the International Animated Film Festival at Annecy in 1985.

Today, Pannonia Film is one of Europe's largest animation production units, and has expanded to include studios in other cities like Kecskemét and Pécs. With its 330 employees, it is able to produce features, television series and advertising spots as well as a steady output of experimental films.

Left: Giacomo Balla's *Dynamism of a Dog on a Leash* (1912); below: Guido Manuli's *Only a Kiss* (1983)

ITALY

The most notable contribution Italian art has made to the twentieth century is arguably the Futurist movement, which began in 1909. Obsessed as the Futurists were by the artistic expression of motion, speed and dynamism of all kinds, one would imagine they were ideally placed to generate an exciting and challenging animation industry in Italy. For instance, notable amongst Futurist artists (such as Balla, Picabia and Carrà) is Umberto Boccioni, who was intensely preoccupied with the treatment of space, form, light and movement. Although, of course, Boccioni's materials were such weighty substances as marble and bronze, every one of the values in his work is shared by creators of animation and film graphics. The Futurists' predominant images were rays of light, arrested gestures and multiple lines, as in paintings like Balla's *Dynamism of a Dog on a Leash* (1912) or Boccioni's statue *Unique Forms of Continuity in Space* (1913). Their work achieved a graphic dimension using multiple viewpoints, vibrations of light, the displacement of objects and fragmentation. Balla's description of the forces which inspired him includes dynamism, colours and luminosity, transformations, drama, noise and explosions. Regrettably, although animation might seem to be the ideal medium for the aesthetics of the Futurist movement, it was never taken up by them as an area for experiment.

Today, Italian animation can be roughly divided into three kinds. In Rome, Emanuele Luzzati and Giulio Gianini (see page 92) are among the leaders of 'decorative art' animation, using vivid colours and a distinctive, fluid style. Also in Rome, Manfredo Manfredi (see page 94) represents the more intensely dramatic style, often using just black and white and myriad shades of grey. In Milan, Bruno Bozzetto (see page 90) and Guido Manuli are prominent figures in the field of animation as comic entertainment.

During the seventies and eighties, many former graphic designers and artists turned their attention to animation, encouraged mainly by the late Professor Ezio Gagliardo of Cinematografica in Rome. Apart from such pioneering work by individuals, however, there is very little support for animation as an art form, especially for a nation with such a considerable tradition of fine art, theatre and cinema.

Below: Peter Foldes' *Visages des Femmes*; bottom: Paul and Gaetan Brizzi's *Asterix in Britain* (1987)

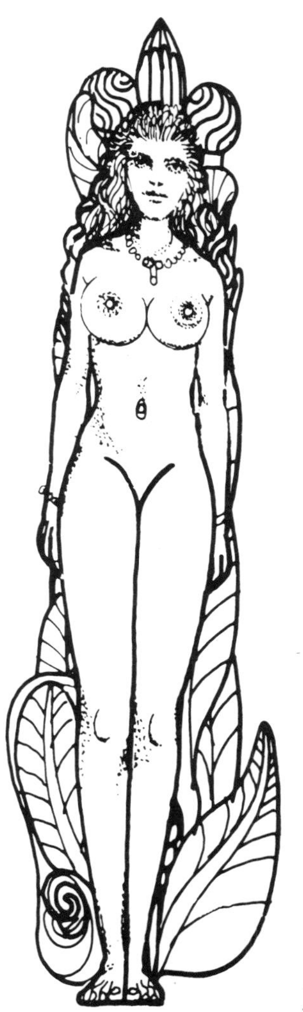

FRANCE

When it comes to the visual arts, France has always boasted a long tradition of excellence, and the history of its animation is no different. The Frenchman Emile Cohl (see page 20) is often regarded as the very first animator and is still internationally renowned for his pioneering achievements. Later, some outstanding artists in France tried their hands at animation, such as Duchamp and Léger, although they (like so many other painters) found the new medium troublesome and complicated when compared with the simplicity of the canvas and paintbrush.

In the late twenties and early thirties in France, the art of animation was mainly practised by a number of immigrant artists. Two Russian animators, Starevitch and Alexeieff (see page 96), an American, Claire Parker (see also page 96), and the Hungarian artist Berthold Bartosch (see page 25) were among the most active practitioners in the field.

French liberalism towards foreign artists was also demonstrated by providing inspiration for a tremendously innovative production, which is still considered a milestone in both graphic art and animation. It was *Joie de Vivre* (1934) by the English painter Anthony Gross and the American Hector Hoppin, and was drawn in simple lines, using a freer graphic style than ever seen in American cartoons. The action consisted of a chase between an Apache-style man on a bicycle and two gracefully drawn Parisienne women.

The commercial side of the animation industry in France was taken up by Ciné Associates and André Sarrut. It was Sarrut who worked on the animated feature-length film project *La Bergère et le Ramoneur* (*The Shepherdess and the Chimney-Sweep*) in the early fifties, with Paul Grimault as director. Grimault (see page 95) was emerging at that time as a major talent and was largely responsible for influencing the course of animation in France.

At around the same time, Jean Image began working in the field, making his first animated feature film in 1953, called *Bonjour Paris*. He sustained a continuous output for several decades. Also in France was Idefix, a company especially formed (under the direction of Albert Uderzo and René Goscinny) to produce Asterix, the famous comic strip character, in the form of animated features. Unfortunately, Idefix only managed to make two Asterix features (in 1967 and 1968) before folding, just as so many other companies had to do through the absence of a large-enough market. The production of Asterix features was resumed, however, by Yannick Piel in 1985, sponsored by Gaumont in Paris. The new studio's second Asterix feature (*Asterix in Britain*) was finished in 1987.

It was French creative talent, however, which went into René Laloux's *La Planète Sauvage*, made in Czechoslovakia, a highly successful animated

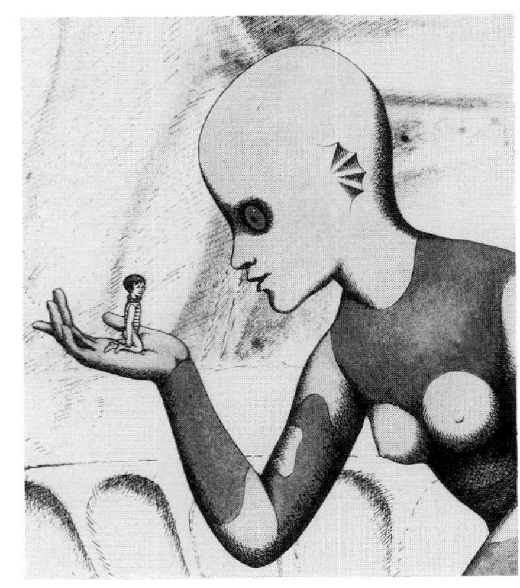

feature film which was in production from 1969 to 1973. Meanwhile, many outstanding artists did their best to struggle along with individually or partially financed films, such as Lenica with *Monsieur Tête* (1959) and Borowczyk with *The Theatre of Monsieur and Madame Kabal* (1967). The Hungarian, Peter Foldes, also came up with a number of highly original films such as *La Belle Cérébrale* (1968) and *Visages des Femmes* (1969).

In the eighties, the French animation industry is in better shape than it has ever been. Government subsidy introduced a modest funding for feature films, a policy which enabled Jean-François Laguionie, for instance (see page 97), to make his beautifully designed film *Gwen* in 1985. Television is also taking notice at last, and several animated series are being initiated, providing popular exposure for animators who are among the best in Europe. In spite of restrictive financial constraints, artists such as Michel Ocelot, Jacques Rouxel and J. C. Villard manage to maintain a standard and variety of styles which distinguish their work amongst modern animators.

CZECHOSLOVAKIA

Between the wars, while animation was blossoming in countries like the USA, Sweden and the USSR, little was happening in Czechoslovakia. There was AFIT in Prague, a studio founded in 1935, which specialised in stop-motion productions, but their products had little originality. The studio was taken over during the German occupation and apart from an indifferent production called *Wedding in the Coral Sea* in 1943 (heavily influenced by Disney), nothing worthwhile emerged. This slow start was quickly compensated for after the war. Several studios were established: Kratky Film, the Trick Brothers' studio and what later became the very well-known Gottwaldov Film Studio. Jiri Trnka (see page 100) was the guiding spirit in Prague and his post-war animated cartoons, *SS* and *Grandpa Planted Turnips*, had a power of expression which soon put Kratky Studio on the map, as did the films of Karel Zeman (see page 98) and the veteran Hermina Tyrlova in Gottwaldov. Hermina Tyrlova's films for children appear simple but the mechanics of production were highly complex. She animated such soft materials as wool, cloth and all sorts of fabrics with a skilful technique which few others have ever mastered. She astounded audiences and delighted children with her approach.

Jiri Trnka's successor as Czechoslovakia's leading figure in animation is Bretislav Pojar (see page 102) who not only inherited Trnka's technique of three-dimensional puppetry but has developed his own system of object animation. Pojar, like his predecessor, maintains his native Czech authenticity but with a universal appeal.

Left: René Laloux's *La Planéte Sauvage* (1973); below left: Michel Ocelot's *La Legende du Pauvre Bossu*; bottom left: Jurišič's *Cock-a-doodle-doo* (1983); right: Jiri Brdecka's *Prince Medenec's Thirteenth Chamber*

There are many other outstanding artists in Prague with their own personalities, such as Stanislav Latal, and Jiri Brdecka with their own brand of visual humour. Also notable are the names of Vaclav Bedrich and the team of Macourek, Doubrava and Born, who have developed a fresh graphic style and a subtlety of criticism about social conditions.

POLAND

There are several elements which distinguish Polish animation from that of other nations. First is the concentration on abstract and graphic formulas as opposed to story-telling, which is often given secondary consideration. An overall theme is usually more important in their films, and this fulfils two functions: it allows graphic visual development to dominate and it maintains the continuity of an idea. The dislike of slapstick and Hollywood-type gags is evident and there are very few physical confrontations or humanised animal characters like Bugs Bunny or Tom and Jerry. Instead there is a deep understanding of human conflict, inner despair and the forces of nature which overwhelm us. Possibly because of frequent wars and the nation's endless suffering between the forces of both East and West, there is a profound sense of melancholy in many of the themes which emerge. However, the potential of the medium is still very much in the foreground, and many Polish animators have a talent for vivid pictorial effects, and possess a poetic imagination.

The Polish animation industry developed soon after the war, and is now divided into several centres of activity: the Se-Ma-For Studios in Warsaw; a Studio at Lodz; one in Bielsko-Biala and another in Poznan. All the units have a high output of films, most of them for children's entertainment.

Among the earliest successes of Polish animation were the productions of Lenica and Borowczyk while they were still in Poland: *Once Upon a Time* (1957) and *Dom* (1958) which they jointly directed before they left for Paris. This film used a predominantly graphic approach in telling a traditional fairy-tale rather than emphasising the narrative, and foreshadowed the style of their joint film *Monsieur Tête* which they made in Paris in 1959 (see page 48). This satire showed Jan Lenica's unique visual style, which undoubtedly makes him one of the most outstanding artists of our time.

Another Polish animator of note is Witold Giersz (see page 103) who used painted graphic spheres and bold brush strokes, showing the variety of pictorial possibilities and solutions in animated films.

Miroslaw Kijowicz, with his films *The Cage* (1966) and later *The Road* (1971), introduced a philosophical element, consciously adopting the simplest line drawing style in order to minimise the visual distractions from the statements made in the films.

Ryszard Czekela, in his 1968 film *Appel* (*Roll Call*), presented a moving depiction of prisoners in a concentration camp who are gunned down by their oppressors. This powerful film, with its half-tone monochrome graphic treatment, provided an unforgettable image.

The animated films of Daniel Szczechura (see page 105) are prime examples of sharp social satire carried out with elegant designs. The comparative newcomer in this distinguished company is Jerzy Kucia (see page 104). Kucia's analytical insect films and glimpses of human behaviour – always observed in closeup from a low camera angle – once again introduce an original visual approach.

The many excellent animated films made in Poland show how a contemporary graphic approach is being kept alive there and the contribution made by Polish animators has substantially enriched the experimental style of animation in Europe.

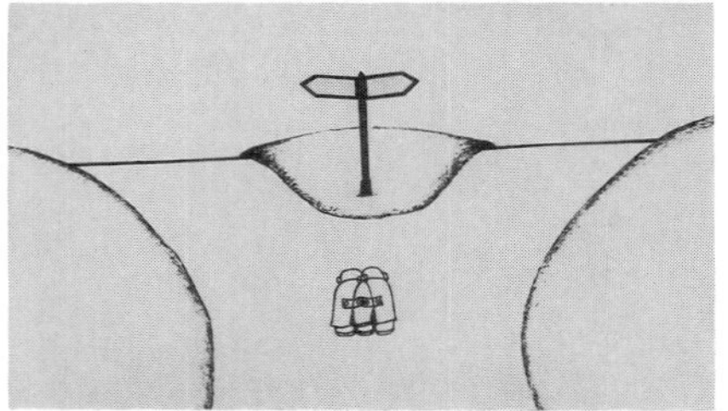

USSR

Activity in the field of animation in the USSR prior to the Revolution of 1917 took place in the studios of Khanzhonkov in Moscow. In 1910, Khanzhonkov invited Ladislas Starevitch from Kovno to work in his studio. The young Starevitch had already established his name as a prodigy in photography and in drawing animals: after joining Khanzhonkov he soon graduated to chief camera operator and animation director. His first experiments were in semi-dimensional relief, a technique which was reintroduced by both Jiri Trnka and Bretislav Pojar in Czechoslovakia in the late fifties.

Starevitch's third film was also in this method, and the result was entitled *The Battle of the Stag Beetles* (1910). The innovative nature of the film was that he seemed to have made the beetles move freely around without any suspension: his complex engineering of wire structures to fix the suspended positions of the beetles was quite ingenious and invisible, as he photographed their positions frame by frame. His other films were on the same

Left: Miroslaw Kijowicz's *The Banner* (1965); below left: Kijowicz's *The Road* (1974)

pattern, and included *Merry Scenes of the Life of Insects* (1912); *Christmas of the Forest Inhabitants* (1911); *The Ant and the Grasshopper* (1911) and *Four Devils* (1913).

Soviet animation in Moscow, however, began to come alive through the work of Ivanov-Vano (see page 106) in the mid-twenties. His version of *The Adventures of Baron Munchausen* in 1929, made in Moscow with Tcherkez and Sutiev, was a large-scale and very popular production. In the same year in Leningrad, Tzekhonovski adapted Marshak's well-known book *The Postman* with a closely synchronised soundtrack for the first time in Russian animation. It was enthusiastically received by both the public and the critics.

There was a healthy expansion in the USSR in the thirties: it was during this period that the careers of the Brumberg Sisters, Anatoli Sazonov and Lev Atamanov began to flourish, serving a growing demand for films for children which were based on traditional Russian fairy-tales. The stories were rich in narrative and characterisation, and usually had a moral to them.

A departure from all this was Alexander Ptushko's *New Gulliver* in 1935, a feature-length puppet film with surprisingly subtle characterisations of political figures, a rarity in the USSR or anywhere else at that time. It had a wide international distribution and was shown in London at the Forum Cinema for a long run in 1936.

In that year Soyuzmultfilm opened in Moscow, but had to restrict its activities due to the threat of war. In the USSR, as in most other countries, animation narrowed its function as an entertainment medium and concentrated on serving the war effort by bringing political posters to life. After the war, the animation industry quickly recovered; while most of Europe's studios suffered from a lack of sponsorship, Russian State subsidy was available to produce a number of feature films.

By that time Soyuzmultfilm Studio in Moscow had become one of the oldest and most active in the field of film animation. Until the beginning of the 1960s their work mainly consisted of the production of animated films for children. The content of these films was intended to both entertain and to influence children's appreciation of moral judgement and ethical values. Clever design and subtle graphic imagery were not considered to be priorities: it was only during the sixties that designers in the USSR began to investigate the potential of animation as a new form of graphic expression, and its possibilities as a form for the visual arts. Since then a gradual shift has taken place both in story content (which became more original and more subtle and began to include hints of sharp human observation) and in pictorial values, which turned into original creative expressions of the individual artist, clearly recognisable for their own style.

In this respect, Russian development kept up with the European breakaway from the Disney concept of realism, by using a style of expression more suited to the genre of film graphics with its possibilities of sharp satire. In the forefront of this movement was Feodor Khitruk (see page

110), whose films appeared in several film festivals in 1963 and won prizes in Oberhausen and San Francisco that same year. Old masters of traditional animation were also inspired by the medium's graphic potential. Ivanov-Vano made films which updated the style of orthodox Russian icons and combined music, movement and colour, creating exciting and authentically Russian films. Yuri Norstein (see page 108) assisted Ivanov-Vano in this work and has since acquired an international reputation as one of the finest contemporary animators. Films made by artists like Serebryakov, Khrzhanovsky and Stepantsev were also much appreciated due to their individual humour, sharp satire and rich textural treatment.

Above: Andrej Khrzhanovsky's *Pushkin* (1983)

In spite of the individual successes of these artists, it would be an exaggeration to say that animation can be used for self-expression to quite the same extent as it can in western Europe or the USA. It is surprising, nonetheless, how liberal the official policy is towards new ideas, provided they attempt to contain some element of audience appeal and story content. In Soyuzmultfilm in Moscow, still the largest studio in the USSR, the working conditions, time devoted to production and the size of budgets are such that most western artists would envy.

The most interesting development over the last years, however, is the rapid spread of studios in the smaller republics. New studios have sprung up in Estonia, Georgia, Latvia, the Ukraine, Kazakhstan, Uzbekistan, Armenia, Azerbaijan, Moldavskaya, Tadzhikistan, Siberia, Byelorussia and Turkmeniya. In the USSR, it appears that, more than any other form of visual communication (including live-action films and television), animation has taken up the development and enrichment of national art and tradition to the extent that it has acquired the status of folk-art itself. Perhaps this will also lead to a broader interchange of national cultures and mutual enrichment beyond the Soviet, Central Asian and Trans-Caucasian nations. At present the work coming out of these studios varies a great deal, depending mainly upon the level of artistic sophistication within a locality. Artists tend to follow regional traditions of age-old national cultures, experience and spirit.

For instance, southern states like Armenia, Kazakhstan and Turkmeniya base their films on the Oriental and Islamic art tradition with highly colourful background designs and 'exotic' characters. In contrast, films from Estonia in the north-west show western European influence in the use of modern designs and abstract forms in the backgrounds. In spite of this, they also manage to maintain a distinctive style of their own.

It is interesting to note that, in many Soviet states, the use of three-dimensional shapes, puppets and marionettes comes as naturally as flat graphic animation. The work of Burovs in the Riga Studio, Rein Raamat (see page 111) and Turganov in Tallinn Film Studio in Estonia, Kistanov of Kazak Films, and Kachanov of Soyuzmultfilm are examples. Just as in Czechoslovakia, it is possible that the tradition to handle puppets is stronger than the use of pencil and brush.

Above: Gerrit van Dijk's *Music for the Millions*; below: Niek Reus' *Jorinde and Joringel*

HOLLAND

The Dutch involvement in animation can be traced back to the middle thirties, when the Hungarian-born George Pal (see page 45) settled in Eindhoven, where he established his puppet studio under the sponsorship of Philips, the international electronics company. Pal made a number of promotional films for Philips, carrying a progressive image of their activities in a universal language which could be understood everywhere in the world. The brilliance of the conceptions, the smooth three-dimensional puppet technique, the charm and humour of the characters and the narratives showing technological development (as in his film *The Ether Ship*) made Pal an outstanding artist and laid the ground for the development of animation in Holland.

One of Pal's collaborators, Joop Geesink, inherited his methods, and opened his own studio which he called 'Dollywood'. Unfortunately, although the skill and performance was technically competent, it could not match Pal's artistry and flair in filmcraft. Others in Holland, however, did better: Toonder, a strip cartoonist, began expanding his work into animation and produced a number of shorts and a feature film, which was quite successful; but it is the younger generation of Dutch animators, perhaps, who contribute most effectively to the art of contemporary animation.

For instance, Paul Driessen (see page 112) is considered to be one of the most original and talented creators of modern animation and has a long list of films to his credit.

Similarly, other Dutch artists, such as Gerrit van Dijk, have produced excellent films with serious social content in a variety of styles like *The Butterfly* and *CubeMenCube*. Borge Ring, a Dane settled in Holland, made two outstanding films: *Oh My Darling* and *Anna and Bella*, which won an Oscar in 1986. Both of these were made in Ring's inimitable, witty style of fluid animation.

Niek Reus belongs to the younger generation of Dutch film artists. He knows the necessities of finding a visual theme for his films, which he carries through with good graphic sense. Holland has a number of talents but, unfortunately, they are still searching for a market and a public for their product. One would have thought that the nation's thriving television industry would be more accommodating.

Right, from top: Ernest and Gisele Ansorge's *Fantasmatic* (Switzerland); Katja Georgi's *Novelle* (East Germany); Raul Garcia-Sanz's *Woman Waiting in a Hotel* (Spain); Ali Akbar Sadeghi's *The Flower Storm* (Iran); Max Bannah's *Violet and Brutal* (Australia)

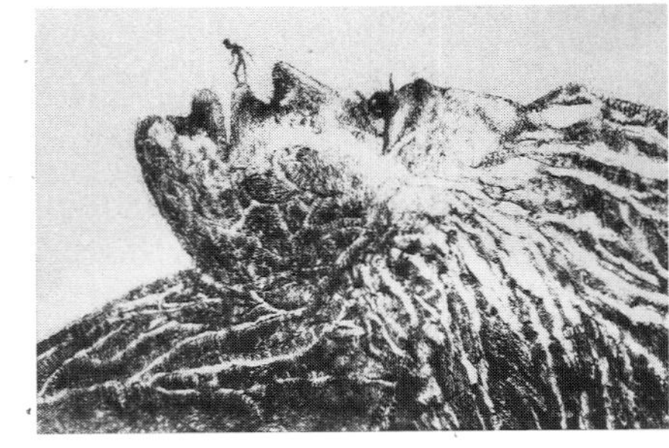

THE OTHER COUNTRIES

To varying degrees, countries like Belgium, Switzerland, Iran, Spain, East Germany, Bulgaria, Romania, Sweden, Finland and Australia have all had intense production activities in several categories of animation.

The immensely talented Ernest and Gisele Ansorge, for instance, working in Lausanne, Switzerland, have specialised in textural animation with crayon and pastel pencils which admirably suits the mythological content of their stories.

In Bulgaria, Todor Dinov, Stoyan Doukov and Donyo Donev have dominated the animation field for the last twenty years. (They are known locally as 'The Three Ds'.) They owe their success to the fact that they are able to bring to the screen folk-tales based on village life, and traditional mystery plays which have considerable power and human interest. They have also utilised traditional songs and music to good effect, providing plenty of colour and nostalgia. Among the new generation of film-makers, Henri Koulev and Roumen Petkov have come up with a wider range of experimental styles and subjects which still have to find acceptance with the general public.

Ion Popescu-Gopo, the Romanian film-maker, had considerable international success with his character, *Homo Sapiens*, his own *alter ego*, who appeared in a number of films, questioning the meaning of human existence. Another of Popescu-Gopo's animated films, *The Apprentice Wizard*, is an excellent manifestation of his skill as a film-maker, combining an animated robot with his own live figure, as the inexperienced robot comes to life in his camera room and destroys the precious equipment.

Scandinavian animation, after such an inspiring start in 1915 by Victor Bergdahl, has so far not lived up to expectations. However, films like Per Åhlin's *Out of an Old Man's Head* and *Thundering Fatty* – both feature-length films – succeeded in generating a lot of interest. Moreover, with a highly-developed television network in Sweden, as well as Film Institutes in Stockholm and Helsinki established specifically to foster film art and culture, it is reasonable to expect some progress from that region.

Animated film prospers in Australia on three different levels. It is extensively used by advertising agencies in the form of television commercials. Several animated feature-length films were produced by Yoram Gross, which successfully survived their test with the public and were very popular. His studio in Sydney employs seventy personnel with the goal of making one animated feature film a year, primarily for the children's entertainment market. There is also a modest activity in short experimental productions, and out of this occasionally surface prize-winning films.

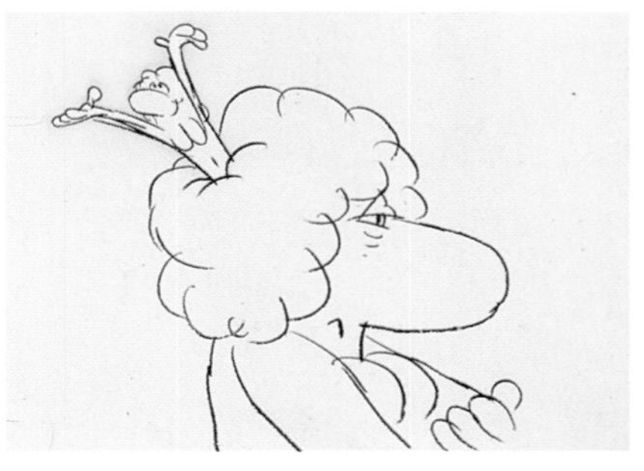

THE MASTERS

WALT DISNEY

Walt Disney was not so much an animator as a phenomenon of the twentieth century. There are a great many books about his life, work and success and he has been called 'the most authentic American genius' whose achievements reveal as much about the America of his time as they do about himself. He has also been called a prudish moralist and a brain manager who harshly exploited the creative talents of other artists to the full: nobody, however, has been able to deny his achievements, his influence, his courage and his consistency.

He was born Walter Elias Disney in 1901 in Chicago and died in December 1966 at Burbank, California, in a hospital opposite his studio. According to Richard Schickel, one of Disney's biographers, it was estimated that in 1966, 240 million people around the world saw a Disney film. Moreover, 100 million watched his television show every week, 800 million read a Disney book or magazine, 50 million listened or danced to his music and records, 80 million bought his licensed merchandise, 150 million read his comic strips and 80 million saw his educational films in churches, clubs and schools. These figures do not include the millions flocking to the theme parks (or outdoor attractions) Disneyland, Walt Disney World and Tokyo Disneyland – and all this began with an unassuming rodent character called Mickey Mouse. One could safely add to Walt Disney's qualifications, therefore, the fact that he was an entrepreneurial genius.

For our purposes, however, it is important to think of 'Disney' not as an individual man but as an animation studio whose work was exemplary in both creative and technical achievement for a long period before it became a commercial enterprise. The Studio had three great assets: Walt Disney's personal talents and ambition, his brother Roy's business acumen, and the brilliance of Ub Iwerks as chief innovator. Disney's early involvement and experimentation with new technical achievements meant that the studio was always in the forefront of animation's development as a medium. With the invention of the talkies, sound effects and music could be added to films in close synchronisation, immeasurably increasing the appeal of the animated cartoon. The two great classics of this period were *Steamboat Willie*, Mickey's début in 1928, and *The Skeleton Dance*, the first of the Silly Symphonies: an inspired piece of Iwerks's choreography using tom-tom beats and xylophones, released in 1929.

The courage and integrity which the Disney brothers displayed when they invested their own money in the first three Mickey Mouse films must be admired. Both the Silly Symphonies and the Mickey films blossomed as the Studio grew and attracted new creative talent. In 1932, Disney was awarded his first Academy Award (Oscar) for *Flowers and Trees*, and by 1934 the now famous Mouse had acquired two new friends, Donald Duck and Goofy, appearing in *The Wise Little Hen* and *Orphans' Benefit* respectively. It was about this time that Disney began to think in terms of full-length animated feature films (see page 33).

The late thirties and early forties were prolific for the Disney Studio, and one feature-length film followed another. The precedent set by the excellent *Snow*

Opposite page, bottom left: *Snow White and the Seven Dwarfs* (1937); bottom right: *Bambi* (1942)
Below: Mickey Mouse in *Fantasia* (1940)

White and the Seven Dwarfs, released in 1937, initiated a spate of successful films including *Dumbo* in 1941 and *Bambi* in 1942. This was interrupted by the entry of the USA into the Second World War, which inspired the war effort and generated several successful propaganda films. When normal activity was resumed, a new generation of classics went into production, culminating in the early fifties with *Cinderella, Alice in Wonderland* and *Peter Pan*. The impressive output continued, the crowning point of which was the feature many critics consider to be the best, *The Jungle Book*, completed in 1967, after Disney's death.

It is believed that Walt Disney was perfectly happy with his studio's artistic style and saw no reason to depart from his established formula. Many critics, however, commented that the 'Disneyfication' of the classics was destroying the literary content and magic of the originals (by authors such as Rudyard Kipling, Lewis Carroll and J. M. Barrie). Generations of children were thought to be growing up with a distorted, sentimentalised idea of some of the great works of children's literature. It was said that, in translating them from one medium to another, he betrayed the spirit of the original, replacing it with jokes and 'fright effects'. No matter: the formula worked and the system achieved enormous popularity with the public.

Other animators never succeeded to the same degree with general audiences, nor with distributors who trusted only Disney products. As an entertainer, he knew how to capitalise on the psychology of children and their parents, and is both heralded as a popular educator and criticised for imposing an overbearing moralism which, it is said, ultimately obscures the real value of his animated cartoons.

Above right: *Pinocchio* (1940); right: *The Jungle Book* (1967)

CHUCK JONES

The work of Chuck Jones provides an illuminating link between animation's past, present and future. With his boundless energy, he is one of the few Hollywood animators who is flexible enough to keep up with the constantly changing styles and techniques.

He is the creative inventor of many popular Hollywood personalities: Bugs Bunny; Porky Pig; Daffy Duck; Pepe le Pew and Elmer Fudd for instance, and such well-known series as *Merrie Melodies*, *Looney Tunes* and *Tom and Jerry*.

He was born in September 1912 in Spokane, Washington. His family moved to Hollywood where he was educated at Hollywood High School, next door to Charlie Chaplin's studio. He maintained that from an early age he learnt a great deal about timing and action from Chaplin. It was comparatively easy to be absorbed into the dynamic expansion of the animated studios of the time, and to work with such talented animators as Hugh Harman, Rudolf Ising, Walter Lantz, Friz Freleng, Bob Clampett and Tex Avery. These animators, along with Max and Dave Fleischer and Walt Disney, were responsible for what is now known as the 'Golden Age of American Cartoons' (see page 25).

After nearly thirty years of feverish activity with others, he finally established his own company, called SIB Tower 12 Productions, to produce a series of *Tom and Jerry* cartoons for MGM which he directed himself. His producer was Les Goldman, who assisted him in making his feature-length film *The Phantom Tollbooth* (1968). His films have so far collected three Oscars and a great number of international awards. Today, still operating from California, he is enjoying his independence by running his own company, producing films for television and cinema and writing about animation. Here are some of Jones's points of view:

'If we ignore our heritage; if we forget or allow to lapse one of the most important factors in the art of pure animation – whether it's a drop of water, a dinosaur, a paramecium, a McLaren dancing line, a blob, a silver wind, a silver flute, a beautifully animated, delightfully floating mass of our own introspection – if we forget that these wonders cannot be accomplished by simple means; if we use limited animation because we can get away with it: then we are overlooking the very essence of our craft and callously destroying history itself.

'We are fortunate, all of us, that animation is so appealing in its versatility. All over the world the most extraordinary things are happening. From Yugoslavia to Japan, South America to, I suppose, Lapland, young men and women are trying new ideas of the most imaginative sort. The medium is springing into life on a thousand fronts with a million facets.'

Above and top left of page: the indomitable Bugs Bunny; left to right: Elmer Fudd; Daffy Duck; Wile E. Coyote; the Road Runner

JOHN AND FAITH HUBLEY

The names of John and Faith Hubley, although less familiar than some, are as significant as any in the development of contemporary animation. Back in the late forties, John Hubley was in the forefront of revolutionising animation by applying a predominantly graphic style in his films, thus updating and upgrading animated cinema to the level of art. He was born in Wisconsin in 1914 and came through the Arts Center in Los Angeles, soon finding a position in the expanding Disney Studio in Burbank. He started as a background painter in the mid-thirties and worked on *Snow White and the Seven Dwarfs*, *Pinocchio*, *Fantasia*, *Dumbo* and *Bambi*.

During the war he worked on instructional films for the animation section of the Air Force in Los Angeles and acquired experience in how to structure animation for a specific purpose. After the war, with other talented young artists such as Steve Bosustow and Bob Cannon, he founded what many now regard as marking a turning point in American animation: United Productions of America (UPA), a studio which has profoundly influenced the range of graphical expression in cartoon animation. Hubley's own contribution included a brilliant parody of the Frankie and Johnny ballad *Rooty Toot Toot*, retelling the fable with his own stylised but penetrating characterisation and fresh, imaginative colour, somewhat resembling a mobile Modigliani. His influence at UPA significantly contributed to the expansion of animation, enabling it to tackle such subjects as James Thurber's *Unicorn in the Garden* and Ludwig Bemelmans's *Madeline*. New ways of dealing with sophisticated satire was the objective, and this talented team found exactly the right graphic approach to convey the stories in movement.

John Hubley left UPA in 1952 to set up his own studio, Storyboard Inc, to produce commercials in an expanding television market. He soon excelled in this field and his television spot for the Ford Motor Company became a classic, as did many of his earlier works. In 1955 he married Faith Elliott, who was at that time a film-music editor and script supervisor in Hollywood. Her energy and imagination regarding subject-matter was the perfect match for John Hubley's style. They continued to explore the visual values inherent in the medium, and consistently produced at least one film each year.

When they married and moved to Faith's home town of New York, a flood of highly original films poured out, among them *The Adventures of an Asterisk* (1956), *The Tender Game* (1958, with the voice of Ella Fitzgerald) and *Moonbird* which won an Oscar in 1960. This stimulated the Hubleys to venture into longer productions like *Of Stars and Men* (1961), an exploration of Man's role in the universe. In 1962 they won another Oscar with *The Hole* using the dialogue of Dizzy Gillespie and George Mathews on the subject of nuclear destruction. Fundamental human problems were the subject of subsequent productions such as *Windy Day* (1968), a child's view of love and marriage; *Of Men and Demons* (1969), on environmental problems; *Eggs* (1971), on fertility and death, and *Voyage to Next* (1974), a comment on the state of humanity. Their last joint film was *A Doonesbury Special* (1977), from Garry Trudeau's comic strip which Faith completed alone when John died in 1977.

Faith continued her work with her rich original style and among many other films directed and produced *WoW* (1975), *Step by Step* (1979), *The Big Bang and Other Creation Myths* (1982) and *Sky Dance* (1982). In 1985 she completed a feature-length film entitled *The Cosmic Eye*.

Above: one of John Hubley's 1950s commercials for Ford Motor Company; right: *A Doonesbury Special* (1977)

Right: *Hello* (1984); below right: *WoW* or *Women of the World* (1975)

The Hubleys made three significant contributions to animation. One: their choice of subject was always guided by conscience regardless of commercial considerations. Two: their style of presentation was closer to that of European Impressionist graphics such as those of Bonnard or Picasso. Three: they pioneered the use of top performers and imaginative dialogue in soundtracks.

Faith: 'I wouldn't do a film I didn't really believe in and love. I've reached the point where if I can't do exactly what I want to do in a film, I'd rather be a bar-tender.'

John: 'Within the growing aggregate of animated film miles each year, I look for new ideas in certain areas of the conceptual process. I am concerned with the move away from comic-strip generalities toward the development of individual human characters. I am also concerned with social criticism; by that I mean the presentation of scenes and problems and dilemmas from ordinary life, and narratives that both please and instruct an audience. These aims seem realisable: to increase awareness; to warn; to humanise; to elevate vision; to suggest goals; to deepen our understanding of ourselves and our relationships with each other.'

BARRIE NELSON

Barrie Nelson is undoubtedly one of the most talented animators to emerge from the crowded field of Hollywood animation during recent decades. He was born in Winnipeg, Canada, in 1933, but has worked in Los Angeles since the 1960s. He followed the school established by the breakaway group of Disney animators (like John Hubley) in the early fifties, and has always had the ability to adapt his style from one storyboard to another. As a freelance animator, this flexibility has proved a great asset and he has been in work constantly since his arrival in America. He has contributed to some outstanding productions including *Windy Day* (1968), *Of Men and Demons* (1969) for John Hubley, and a *Peanuts* feature directed by Bill Melendez, in 1970.

Nelson has also been enterprising enough to make and finance his own productions, which is not a universal practice. His first attempt as director/producer was *Keep Cool* in 1972, which became a prize-winner at the Zagreb Animated Film Festival. His second attempt was *Twins* in 1974 and his third, entitled *Opens Wednesday* (1979), was jointly financed by an American Film Institute grant and himself. With Nelson acting as writer, designer, director, animator and producer, *Opens Wednesday* is possibly his best and most individual work to date. The main character of this film is an ironic self-portrait: an authoritarian cartoon director creating his cartoon and visual gags on the screen, commenting on the slowness of the action and wilfully speeding it up like a tyrannical conductor of an orchestra. It also contains some surprises of juxtaposition and metamorphoses, all of which are only possible through the medium of animation. The film is very funny, not because of routine physical confrontations on which many productions depend but because of the treatment of abstract ideas.

During recent years he has, among other things, directed and animated a film called *You Can't Teach an Old Dog New Tricks*. It was produced by the sound-and-voice queen of Hollywood cartoons, June Foray, and is about the relationship between a lecherous old man and a glamorous Hollywood starlet.

Left: *Opens Wednesday* (1979); below left: *Keep Cool* (1972); below and bottom: *You Can't Teach an Old Dog New Tricks* (1984)

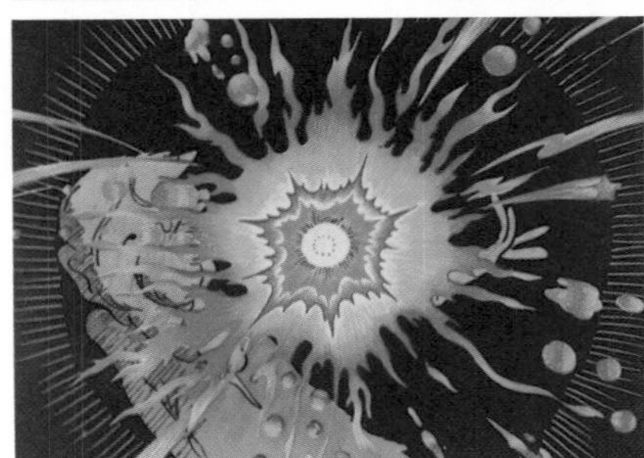

CAROLINE LEAF

Caroline Leaf entered animation when she took some courses with Derek Lamb, an English-born animation pioneer at Harvard University's Carpenter Center for Visual Arts. Her original approach to film-making emerged immediately. Instead of using conventional tools she experimented with materials such as sand on a light box. By spreading this onto transparent glass she created layers of tones which were then filmed from above. The thickness of the sand was adjusted by adding or thinning out the layers. With the right illumination, the tonal quality could be varied from pure black to half-tones. Movement was advanced by adding or subtracting the sand. She experimented with this method and eventually attained perfection, being able to apply total control over the material. Her art is through her fingertips. She describes her work as follows:

'I found I could adequately describe a form by its silhouette. The only elements I had were black and white, figure and ground. When the options are limited my fantasy is at its most creative to exploit them.'

She was born in Seattle, USA, in 1946 and joined the National Film Board of Canada in 1972. One of her first assignments was a film based on an Eskimo legend. The Canadian Film Board's objective was to present an interpretation of Canada to Canadians at home and abroad, and in the course of her studies Leaf came across the Eskimo story, which she eventually used, called *The Owl Who Married a Goose* (1974). On Holman Island, in the Western Arctic, she worked with Nanogak, an Eskimo woman artist with whom she created the storyboard. The film was made back in Montreal with her system of animating with sand, taking a year and a half to produce. For the sound she returned to the Arctic where her Eskimo friends supplied the soundtrack in the form of 'throat music', thus retaining the original atmosphere of the project. *Owl* turned out to be something of a masterpiece. One image or situation melts into another with a superb fluidity of motion and its tonal beauty is a visual delight. After five more films using the sand medium she made the award-winning film *The Street*, using a slightly more complex but related technique. She worked with inks, finger-painting onto a sheet of glass, this time introducing colour, which she used with the utmost discretion. She controlled the animation by endlessly erasing and repainting the figures on the glass. The motion advances effortlessly with a smooth continuity, blending, shaping, transforming; taking the audience through the highly dramatic story-line. The narrative is imaginatively interpreted, with constant surprises and detailed visual concepts about the habits of its main characters. The film deservedly won an Oscar in 1977.

Her next film was an animated version of Kafka's *Metamorphosis of Mr Samsa* (1977) – an allegorical fantasy which was entirely suited to her artistic style and technique. One of her recent films is an interpretation of *The Owl and the Pussycat* (1985), providing more evidence that it is the natural fusion of style and substance in her films which makes her one of the most interesting artists in animation today.

Below: *The Street* (1976); below left: *The Owl Who Married a Goose* (1974)

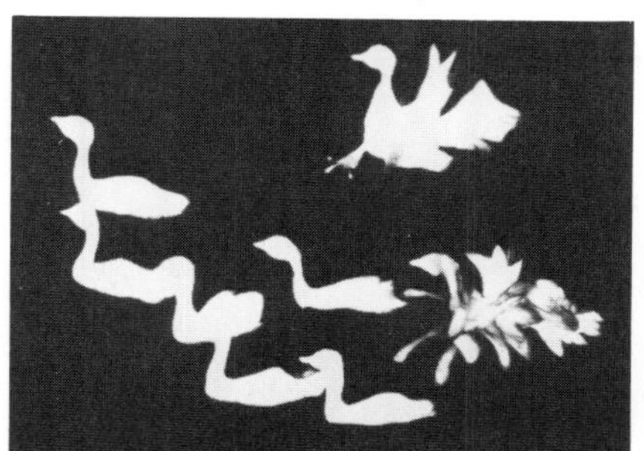

NORMAN McLAREN

Norman McLaren has been in the forefront of animated art since before the war. His achievements have been characterised by his creative and technical brilliance and by his sensitivity to the human condition. This was manifested particularly in his attitude towards the underdeveloped countries in Asia, where he spent a period of time helping to eradicate illiteracy by means of his visually orientated methods of reading and writing.

McLaren was born in Stirling, Scotland, in 1914. At the age of eighteen he began a five-year course at the Glasgow School of Art, specialising, during his last three years, in interior design. He started making films in 1934 and entered two in a Scottish amateur film festival where they not only won awards but also captured the attention of John Grierson the adjudicator. Impressed by McLaren's talent he offered him a job at the General Post Office film unit in London. In 1936, during the Spanish Civil War, McLaren worked as a cameraman in Spain. In 1939, sensing the approach of another war and still haunted by his Spanish experience, he left England and arrived in New York. In 1941, at the invitation of John Grierson (by then Canada's first Government Film Commissioner), McLaren left New York to join the National Film Board of Canada. The association was a spectacular success from the start. With his innovative style of drawing and painting onto the raw material of the film stock, McLaren made a number of highly original short films to help the Canadian war effort. *Dollar Dance* and *Fiddle-de-Dee* combined propaganda with entertainment and soon McLaren established himself as the most useful and original artist of the Board.

He is an exceptional artist who regards himself as a research worker in film techniques. He is particularly fascinated by music and the relationship of soundtrack to visuals and claims that in many of his films the actual starting point was music, as in *Fiddle-de-Dee* (1947), *Begone Dull Care* (1949) and *La Merle* (1958), as well as those which have folk-music as their basis. His ambition is to create a totally wordless film that is based on mime or dance. Abstract films, he believes, may only contain unrepresentative shapes but since they assume motion in time and space they can possess a great deal of humanity.

McLaren's films are based more on movement than colour and in many of his films colour is only introduced at a later stage to heighten the emotional effect. In *La Poulette Grise* (1947) the action was advanced through a series of dissolves and the building up of pastel drawings, which depended upon extremely subtle shades of colour.

His innovations have astonished the animation world, bringing to life inanimate objects, as in *A Chairy Tale* (1957), and scratching, drawing and painting directly onto the raw film stock to explore the dynamics of motion, as in *Blinkity Blank* (1959). In *Pas de Deux* (1968) and *Narcissus* (1983) he experimented with live-action film of ballet dancers, step-printing their movements using optical printers. Each graceful gesture was separated into a sequence of minute movements which overlapped, creating an exquisite and ghostly visual effect.

In his first years at the National Film Board of Canada, McLaren was given the task of organising an animation studio. Over the ensuing years, his work has encouraged and inspired many award-winning film-makers and the subsequent success of the new generation of Canadian animators has, to some extent, been due to his patience and example.

Left: sequence from *Blinkity Blank* (1959); below: *Neighbours* (1952); opposite page, top and bottom: *Pas de Deux* (1968)

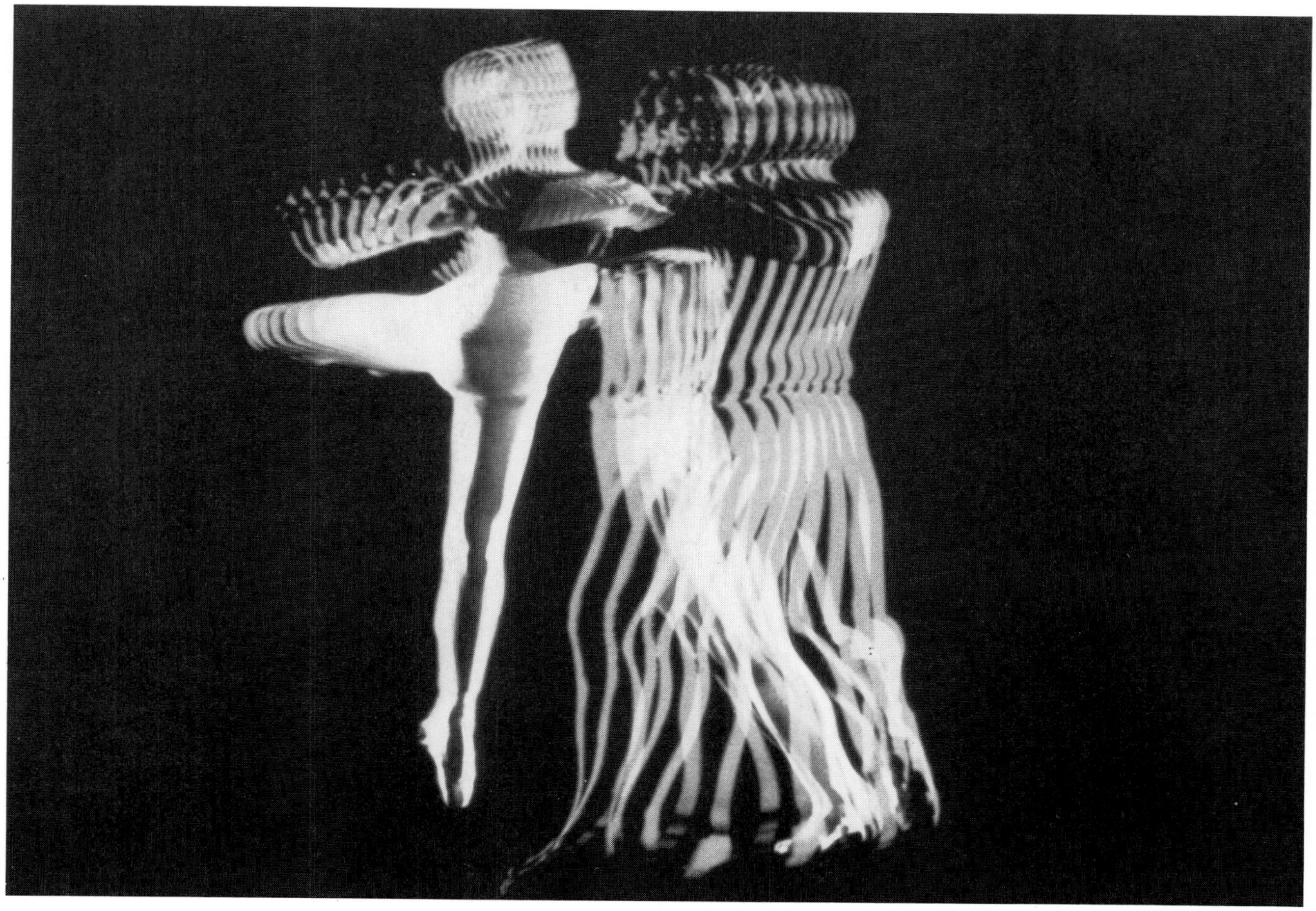

FRÉDÉRIC BACK

Frédéric Back is a quiet, unassuming man: that is, until he starts to discuss animation. Then he blossoms into an exuberant human being who is obviously in complete command of his medium. His mastery of timing, his elegant but simple design, his characterisation and observation of animated figures – especially children – and his stories, which are written with a warm sense of humanity, make him an all-round professional.

He was born in Saarbrücken, West Germany, in 1924 and spent his youth in Strasbourg. He studied art in Paris and Rennes and was a student of the marine painter Méheut. His early work was exhibited in Paris and Rennes.

After he settled in Montreal in 1948 he soon became a Professor at the School of Furniture Design and later in the School of Applied Arts and the School of Fine Arts. His first entry into film and television was in 1952 when he joined the graphic arts department of the Canadian Broadcasting Corporation. From this position he had an opportunity to research into the production processes of painting onto glass, which led him to the art of stained-glass window design. The radiant luminosity of his films possibly comes from this early interest.

In 1968 he moved into the animation department of CBC and he has had a close working contact with the department's director, Hubert Tison, ever since. This co-operation has met with world-wide success for all parties: CBC, Tison and Frédéric Back, who has since become a Canadian citizen.

His films, among them *La Création des Oiseaux* (1973), *Illusion* (1974), *Taratata* (1977) and *Tout Rien* (1978), have won him several international prizes and have helped him and other talented artists establish the animation department of CBC as one of the best in North America.

Possibly the summit of Back's success, however, was *Crac!* in 1980, a nostalgic tale of an old rocking-chair which won the 1982 Oscar for Best Animated Film.

The success of Back's films lies in their emotional treatment, which generates human sympathy and a love of nature. If these themes were handled by anyone else, they could become mere sentimental clichés, but in the hands of Frédéric Back they emerge as inspired and good-humoured entertainments which appeal strongly to children. And one can see why children love his films. *Taratata* and *Tout Rien*, for example, look at festivity and fantasy from a child's perspective, using magical colours, metamorphosis and an optimistic vision which says that anything is possible.

Above right: *La Création des Oiseaux* (1973); right: *Tout Rien* (1978); below: *Crac!* (1980); opposite page: *Taratata* (1977)

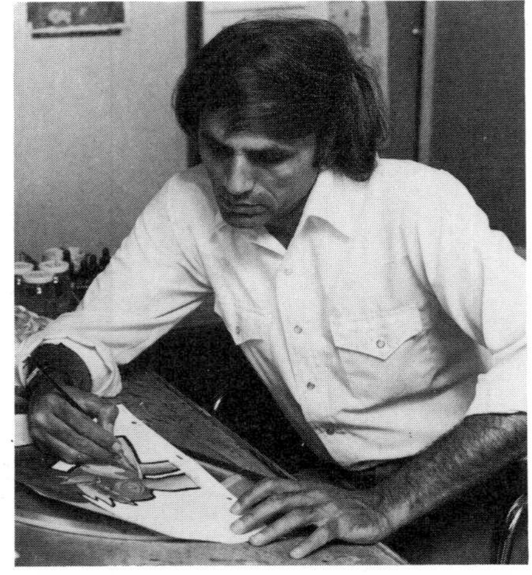

ISHU PATEL

Ishu Patel has a unique visual language through which he expresses a personal style which is rich and colourful. His work is markedly different from the more graphic approach taken by the majority of European animators, and he brings to animation a splendour, sparkle and a wealth of oriental imagery that is reminiscent of Indian miniature painting.

Born in 1942 in India, Patel has been working for the National Film Board of Canada for several years, during which time he has made a number of highly original and memorable films. They include: *How Death Came to Earth* (1971); *Bead Game* (1977); *Afterlife* (1978); and his most recent film *Paradise* (1985). As one might guess from the titles, the content of his films is as unusual as his visual treatment of them, attempting to explore and celebrate the spiritual mysticism of the Orient.

In *Paradise*, for instance, he shows the magical self-transformation of a blackbird for his Emperor. The blackbird despises his own natural paradise and spurns his companions, plundering their nests to make himself into a clown-like imitation of the Divine Bird, pleading for the favour of the Emperor. The unfortunate bird, however, fails to impress and is imprisoned outside the palace walls. This ancient Indian tale is carried through in a splendid style, conveying a wealth of visual beauty which is largely achieved by effective and highly decorative underlighting. The crystal palace is created without painted backgrounds: the brilliant effects are achieved by piercing the paper and letting the light penetrate through. To create the final touch, a star-filter is used on the lens which splits the light coming through each tiny hole into a star-shaped beam which creates a haze and glitter to the background. In order to achieve the final effect, each scene had to be re-shot between five and twenty-four times. Ishu Patel states:

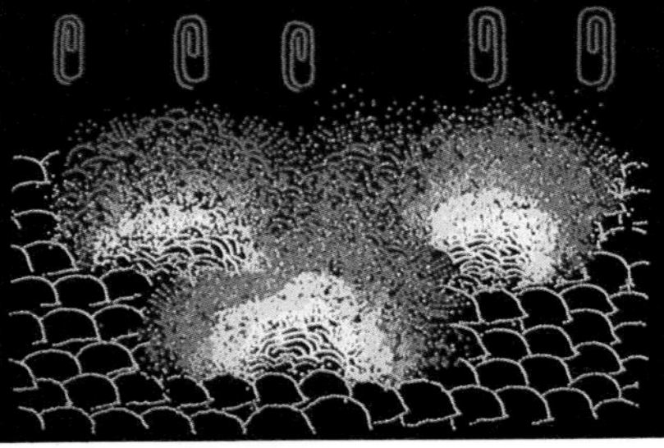

'No matter how well off we are, when we see others with greater wealth or comfort we feel deprived and envious.'

Patel is a shrewd observer of human weaknesses and greed and this perception pervades the content of his films, just as his elegant artistry determines their distinctive style.

KIHACHIRO KAWAMOTO

One of the most original animators to emerge from Japan during the last decade is Kihachiro Kawamoto, the puppet-film animator. He is entirely devoted to his work, which he controls from the story concept to the design of his figures, which he himself arranges for the camera. He also prefers to sew the figures' costumes himself.

Kawamoto was born in Tokyo, Japan, in 1924. His ambition was originally to become an architect, since it would have been difficult to have made a living in wartime conditions as a puppeteer. After the war, however, at the age of twenty, he found employment with the Toho Film Studio designing sets, a job lasting four years. His first introduction to animation was when the famous Czechoslovak puppet-film director, Jiri Trnka, visited Tokyo and presented his film *The Emperor's Nightingale* (1948). Kawamoto was spellbound and decided to follow the great master. He went to Europe, studied puppetry with Trnka in Czechoslovakia and later continued his work in Hungary, Romania, Poland and Russia.

It wasn't easy to establish himself back in Japan. The structure of the Japanese animation industry is based on a factory system supplying animated films for children in vast quantities. An independent artist is an outsider. Nevertheless, Kawamoto was able to make a number of outstanding short films such as *Farce Anthropocynique* (1971), *Demon* (1972), *A Poet's Life* (1974), *Dojoji* (1976) and *House of Flame* (1979). The last two combine many of his best talents: brilliant design of traditional puppets; plasticity – which has established him as a unique artist; expert story-telling and first-class colour sense. These are universal qualities which have been recognised by the great number of international awards he has received.

Artistically, his roots are in the great puppet tradition of Japan which began during the Edo era in the seventeenth century. At that time, art was a popular culture and puppet performances were very much a part of it. Originally, the puppets were worked at the end of the arm and as the form developed, several could be manipulated at the same time. Bunraku and the famous Kabuki theatre emerged later, with their traditional repertory.

With the influx of Western culture, the tradition of Japanese puppetry declined. In this century the two styles co-existed for a time, through the traditional Bunraku and modern puppets.

Below: *Demon* (1972); opposite page, left: Patel's *Bead Game* (1977); below left: *Paradise* (1985)

Kawamoto is on his way to reviving both traditions by expanding them in the new format of motion pictures. He utilises the essence of their visual images in a streamlined form and bases his stories on the traditional 'Jojuri' performances which involve the participation of mythical gods, humans and spirits. He states:

'The creation of a single puppet takes ten days. The head requires particular care. First I prepare a plaster mould with which I fashion the head from an agglomerate of Japanese paper, which is then covered with a fine supple leather and subsequently painted; thus it is light but solid. Eyes, mouth and eyebrows are moveable, and the ears, in plastic, are made from moulds which I myself fashion. Teeth are fashioned from a type of paraffin, the chests from rigid paper; the hands, in supple rubber, are easily moved. For ten minutes of animation one year of preparation is required.

'What interests me most in the production of animated film is that the person who creates it is the only one who can express what he feels, like a painter.'

Right: *Dojoji* (1976); above right: *House of Flame* (1979); above: *A Poet's Life* (1974); opposite page: Kinoshita's *Japonese* (1977)

RENZO KINOSHITA

Renzo Kinoshita made his name with a satirical film about modern Japan entitled *Japonese* (1977). His sharp observation about the brutalities of mechanised Japan attracted the attention of both the public and the jurors at the International Film Festival in Leipzig, East Germany, where I first met him in 1972. Prior to this, however, he had already established himself in Japan in the commercial field as well as with experimental short films produced with his wife Sayoko, who is also an accomplished artist.

Renzo Kinoshita was born in Osaka, Japan, in 1936. As a young boy during the early post-war period he was an ardent fan of American and Japanese comic books by such popular artists as Fukujiro Yokoi and Osamu Tezuka. After graduating from High School in 1956, he was determined to try his hand at animation, like so many others who were impressed with the early Disney features, notably *Fantasia*. He eventually found a job in Osaka with Ikko, a busy commercial studio where he had plenty of opportunity to pick up the tools of the trade. At Ikko he worked with Tsunoyama Kimura, whose influence made him determined to pursue his career in animation.

Today he is one of the few all-round animators in Japan functioning independently. After a period with Tezuka's Mushi Productions in Tokyo, he formed his own studio, Lotus, with his wife in 1960. As in the USA, to survive in a commercial climate is a major achievement and mass-produced series for children's television dominate the market.

The Kinoshitas' best-known film, *Pica Don* (1978), for instance, could never have been made in a commercial studio, since it would not fit into the conveyor-belt system. Its content, the destruction of human life through the bomb at Hiroshima, is still a very sensitive and painful subject in Japan. Renzo and Sayoko Kinoshita bravely tackled the problem after studying the paintings of the survivors left behind in Hiroshima. It is an extremely moving and powerful film, showing the life of the inhabitants before the event and the devastating effect of the destruction afterwards. The intention was to convey the experience as subjectively as possible with the hope that it should never happen again. The treatment of the film at the beginning is gentle, showing normal life in the community, but culminates in horror, taking on a grotesque visual style wholly appropriate to the inhumane subject-matter. With its competent graphic style and excellent animation it succeeds as a major warning carried out in a highly artistic form.

Far left: a storyboard for *Pica Don* (1978); left: four of the finished scenes; opposite page, right: Tezuka's *One Thousand and One Nights* (1969); above right: a cartoon self-portrait

OSAMU TEZUKA

Osamu Tezuka's background is the world of comic strips and comic books. He is a fantastically versatile artist who can adapt easily from book illustration to writing and drawing comics, or to film production. He is also able to produce both experimental productions and films designed to appeal to popular audiences. His experiments are based more on story invention than on technical innovations, but both activities benefit from a desire to achieve a high standard of craftsmanship. He can combine a traditional Japanese design with another, more universal style, which explains why he is so popular both in his own country and internationally.

He was born in Osaka, Japan, in November 1926. From an early age he was fascinated by comic books and soon became an admirer of the early Donald Duck, Popeye and Felix the Cat films. His addiction to drawing cartoons was discouraged by his teachers, which only made him even more determined to pursue the subject. His parents, however, wanted him to enter the medical profession so he studied medicine at the University of Osaka, where he took a doctorate in Human Anatomy.

Nevertheless, Dr Tezuka preferred to go back to his favourite pursuit and soon became a political cartoonist for national newspapers. In addition he joined Japan's largest animation studio, Toei, where he was soon asked to direct full-length feature films, such as *Alakazam the Great* in 1960 and the highly popular series *Astro Boy* in 1963.

In 1962 he began his company, Mushi Productions Inc, which mushroomed into a unit of 500 personnel working under a great deal of pressure from both management and the unionised staff. Eventually he started his own unit, Tezuka Productions, in 1970.

During the Mushi Productions period he directed a number of expensive feature films, among them *One Thousand*

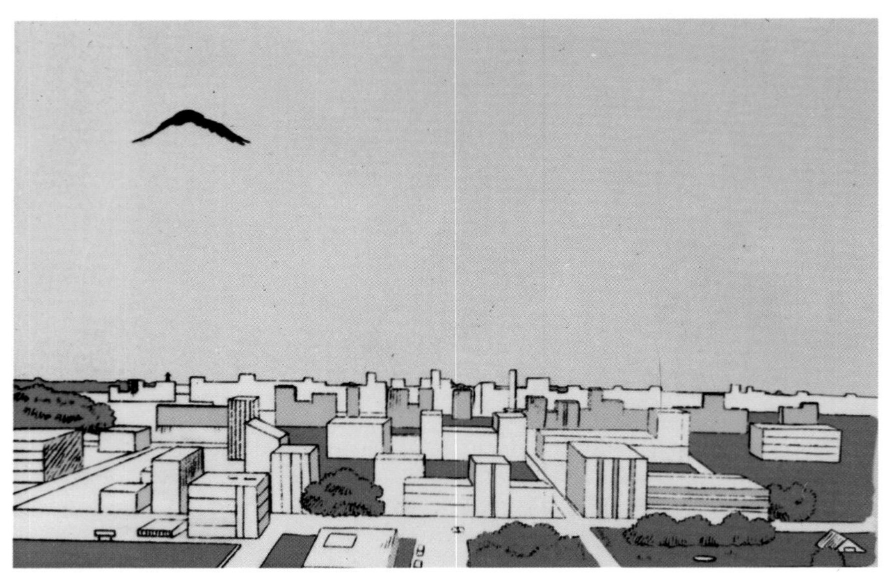

Three aerial views from *Jumping* (1984)

watched the earth recede and advance as they themselves apparently 'jumped'. Tezuka's film, which turns the action into a subjective experience, is not the only attempt at this, but certainly one of the finest examples of it. The attention to detail is impeccable, and the sequential movements entirely believable.

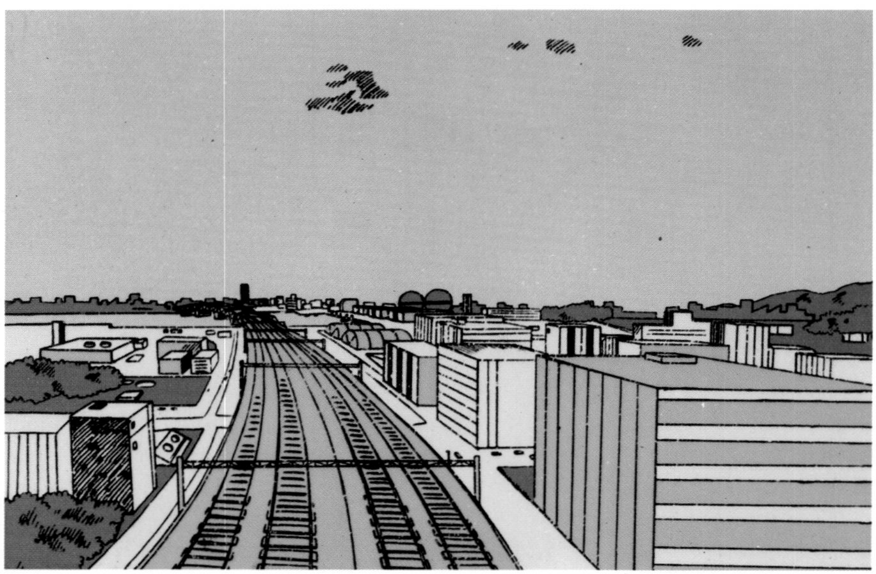

and One Nights (1969) and *Cleopatra* (1970) which pleased both critics and audiences around the world. The design was distinguished and the technical merits quite astonishing for a company working under strict commercial circumstances.

Since he became independent, the prolific Dr Tezuka has written and produced a great number of books for children and adults and made high-quality short films, among them *Jumping* which won the Grand Prix at the Zagreb International Film Festival in 1984. This film reveals Tezuka in a totally new role, that of humorist and experimentalist. What he did was radically alter the perspective of the audience – they did not watch someone else jump hundreds of feet in the air, crossing oceans in a single leap; they

DUŠAN VUKOTIĆ

The name of Dušan Vukotić is inseparable from the development of the Zagreb Animated Film Studio and its world-wide reputation. He was born in 1927 in Montenegro, Yugoslavia. He studied architecture in Zagreb and worked for some time as a caricaturist on the humorous magazine *Kerempuh*.

In 1951 Duga Film was founded, the first Yugoslav studio for the production of animated film, and Vukotić began making his first two-reel animated film there in 1951. Even in his first films made in black and white, his search for self-definition and an expression of his own vision of animated film is clearly evident. When Duga Film ceased to exist for economic reasons, Vukotić and a group of colleagues and enthusiasts founded a new animation studio within Zagreb Film in 1956. This very quickly became known as the world-renowned Zagreb School of animation.

The versatile Vukotić has made many animated films, assuming the roles of scriptwriter, director, chief designer and chief animator. He also made several animated documentary and educational films and directed a combined animation/live-action feature film for children called *The Seventh Continent*.

Vukotić has developed a formula combining simple expressive graphics with amusing calligraphy which imaginatively utilises the medium of animation, and he has a sense of timing which is usually only seen in slick animated films from Hollywood. He is in total control of his material, a clever director who knows how to manipulate the technical resources available to him. He also knows exactly how to structure a film and where to put the major emphasis to create the desired atmosphere. His films have received over eighty international awards and diplomas in various film festivals throughout the world. In 1958 he made a notable film called *Concerto for Sub-Machine-Gun*, successfully combining surrealism with excellent character animation and making strong use of the soundtrack, expert timing and design. His film *Piccolo* (1959) was selected by the British Film Academy as the best animated film to be shown during 1960. He also made *The Cow on the Moon* in 1959 and *Ersatz* in 1961, which in 1962 became the first animated film by a director outside the USA to win an Oscar. His film *The Play* (1962) was a production which combined live-action and animated film and was about the fierce confrontation between two children.

Below: *Concerto for Sub-Machine-Gun* (1958); bottom: *Piccolo* (1959)

NEDELJKO DRAGIC

Nedeljko Dragic's dynamic energy is such that many people have difficulty keeping up with it. Fortunately, when it comes to animation he knows exactly when to take a breath and allow his audience to catch up before he leaps forward once again. He is essentially a comedian of abstract images portraying the human condition via his imaginative cartoons.

Dragic was born in 1936 in Paklenica, Yugoslavia. He studied law in Zagreb before becoming a newspaper cartoonist in 1953 and has been working on animated films since 1960 with Zagreb Animated Film Studio. In 1964 he also published a book of his cartoons, *Alphabet for Illiterates*, and since then he has won numerous awards for his anti-heroic comic strips including first prize at the Montreal Festival of 1971 for his strip *Tupko*.

So far, Dragic has been responsible for some thirty films, but during the first period of his career with Zagreb Film he was acting as designer; it was not until 1965 with the film *Elegy* that he became a director. He had a substantial success during the 1966 Annecy Film Festival in France in winning the Grand Prix with his film *Tamer of Wild Horses*. The horses possessed a physical power seldom experienced in any film, live or animated. His next film, *Diogenes Perhaps* (1967), won a Gold Medal in the Belgrade Festival in Yugoslavia.

In his film *Tup Tup* (1972), the 'human condition' he deals with is the universal – and comical – pursuit of the female by the male and vice versa. It has such a fast pace, however, that the details are of little consequence: it is the overall effect which matters. In *Diary* (1974), possibly his best film, he breaks new ground. It is a record of his impressions, dreams and hallucinations over the period of a year, expressed in the form of visual images. Among them is the sinking of New York's island of Manhattan into the sea; as the water gobbles up the island we feel that the whole of 'civilisation' is disappearing and sinking into the sea. The impression is pure visual magic; he profoundly understands how animated design should be integrated with sound effects and music and how to appeal to both the intellect and the emotions of the audience.

Left, right and below: a man and his symbols – Dragic's animated subconscious in *Diary* (1974); above right: *The Day I Stopped Smoking* (1982)

OUR
WORLD
WES

BORIVOJ DOVNIKOVIĆ

Some artists enter into film animation circuitously, often after first trying their hand at fine art or graphic design. In contrast, Borivoj Dovniković went straight for the field of cartoon animation almost instinctively.

Dovniković is a caricaturist with a strong natural talent: an observer of human weaknesses and comic situations resulting from greed, stupidity and domination. He is a fearless critic of any tradition or custom which blocks freedom of expression or action, but he is never malicious and never revolutionary in the political sense. His sharp but humorous observations contain an element of comic entertainment which is designed to reveal to the audience its own absurdities, thus educating and, potentially, reforming the spectators.

Dovniković was born in Osijek, Yugoslavia, in 1930. Immediately after the war he studied at the Zagreb Academy of Fine Arts. While still studying there, he began to contribute caricatures to popular comic magazines: the money earned was invested in cartoon film production. It was through his amateur activities that he acquired some basic experience in the complex technical processes of film production. Later he found it easy to adapt his strip cartoon characters to moving ones, particularly since he had been in the habit of drawing figures from the age of three and redrawing them whenever he found a piece of paper. As a constant admirer of moving pictures his ambition was realised when the first opportunity came along to make a cartoon film with his already popular comic strip character Kerempuh.

The production of his first epic took much longer than anticipated. He finished it in one year: it was a political satire lasting twenty minutes entitled *A Big Rally* and helped to establish the first Yugoslav animated film studio, Duga Film, in 1951.

After returning to comic strip cartoons for a while, Dovniković joined Zagreb Film, a newly established studio, in 1958. It was at that time the cradle of the famous Zagreb School of Animation, which later became world famous through the brilliant work of Dovniković and his colleagues Mimica, Vukotić, Kostelac, Kristl, Grgic and others. He fitted into this distinguished company admirably, contributing his own special talents to help make Zagreb Film appreciated on an international level.

His 1961 film *A Doll* collected many diplomas and prizes and as time went on his films went from strength to strength. *Second-Class Passenger* (1973) is a classic work on snobbery, while *Learning to Walk* (1978) investigates the complexities of what lies behind an ordinary man with an 'instinct' for domination, violence and selfishness. Herein lies the illusion of Dovniković's art. His characters appear straightforward, even innocent, but inside they are often aggressive animals, confronted with a corrupt society, and become victims of their own self-indulgence. This is what emerges in most of his films, especially in *One Day of Life* (1982) which is undoubtedly a minor masterpiece.

Below left: *Second-Class Passenger* (1973); below: *One Day of Life* (1982)

BOB GODFREY

It could be said that Bob Godfrey is to British animation what *The Goon Show* was to British radio: typifying the irreverent, anarchic side of a generation of British humour. Early on, Godfrey introduced these elements into his films, gleefully expanding them with animated movement.

He was born in Australia of British parents in 1921, and was educated and brought up in England. His first regular employment was with the W. M. Larkins studio in London, and after a period of five years he started the Biographic Studio with other colleagues before forming his own unit, Bob Godfrey Films, in 1965. During the Biographic days, his two most notable films were *Polygamous Polonius* (1958), an ingenious and very funny film about sex, and *The Do-It-Yourself Cartoon Kit* (1959).

As an entirely independent producer and animator, Godfrey has maintained three quite different types of animated film in which to channel his energy. One group is represented by *L'Art pour L'Art* (1965), *Rope Trick* (1967) and *Great*, his Oscar-winning film on the genius of the British engineer Brunel, made in 1975. Another group is composed of his numerous parodies on sex, including: *Henry 9 'Till 5* (1969); *Kama Sutra Rides Again* (1971); *Dream Doll* (1979); *Instant Sex* (1980) and *Bio Woman* (1981). *Dream Doll*, which he co-directed with the Yugoslav Zlatko Grgic, was nominated for an Oscar and a British Academy Award. His other highly successful group is for television, with two series for children, *Roobarb* (1974) and *Henry's Cat* (1983), the latter now in its third series.

Bob Godfrey is recognised and acclaimed as a natural comic and animator, with an instinct for sharp (but harmless) parody: the overall texture of his films is humorous and gently anti-establishment. He enjoys an international reputation as an imaginative artist and a good teacher. He is also the co-Chairman of the Education Commission and a Director of the Executive Board of the International Animated Film Association.

Below: *Great* (1975); bottom: *Dream Doll* (1979)

GEORGE DUNNING

Few artists have contributed more to the modernisation of animated film than George Dunning. He was among those artists who entered on the crest of the new wave in animation which revolutionised the medium at the end of the war. His quick wit was nearer to English humour than his own native Canadian and the sense of design with which he expressed his visual poetry in *The Tempest* made an outstanding contribution to the world of animated film-making.

George Dunning was born in Toronto, Canada, in 1920. He joined the National Film Board of Canada in 1942, where he worked with Norman McLaren and met Alexandre Alexeieff, who was at that time a visiting artist from Paris. The influence of both these experimental artists on the young Dunning is clearly evident in his early work before he found his own style.

An early film was a black and white paper-cut-out experiment made in 1944 called *Grim Pastures*. It was followed by *Three Blind Mice* (1945) and *Cadet Rousselle* (1946), the latter based on a traditional folk-song.

A turning point for Dunning, though, was in 1955 when he joined the United Productions of America unit in New York and worked on the 'Gerald McBoing Boing' series for six months. This series had a continuously humorous story-line based on visual gags and was produced for television. He undertook to represent UPA in London in 1956 where the market for television commercials was expanding, and soon formed his own company, TV Cartoons, with some of the UPA personnel. A number of notable productions came out from this new unit in addition to serving the commercial television market, *The Wardrobe* (1959), *The Apple* (1962) and *The Ladder* (1964) among them. But the real breakthrough was in 1962 with *The Flying Man*, based on Stan Hayward's story and winner of the Grand Prix, Annecy, 1962, which was directly animated with bold, fluid brush strokes. This style of animation was a relief from the heavy-handed, factory-made cartoons which flooded television screens at that time.

The enchanting production of *Yellow Submarine*, using the familiar music of the Beatles in their prime, came along during 1968. Many 'Flying Man' techniques were applied in this eighty-minute feature film which used several experimental graphic techniques. The lessons learnt from television commercials had been cleverly made use of in this feature, which is sometimes considered to be a catalogue of the graphic styles of the late sixties. Heinz Edelmann's design gave the film a sense of surrealism and freshness which has a lasting value, far outweighing its period look.

After *Yellow Submarine* he directed three notable short films, *Moon Rock* (1970), *Damon the Mower* (1971) and *The Maggot* (1972), the latter being a powerful work on drug abuse. With his simple, elegant drawing style and thorough understanding of the basic roots of animation, Dunning made a significant contribution to its development as an exciting and intelligent medium for the graphic arts.

Sadly, he died in London in 1979. His ambition had been to translate Shakespeare's *The Tempest* into an animated film, but he managed to finish only four minutes of it in colour. The rest could never be completed, since both the style and the design bore his unique personal touch. He described his approach as follows:

'I've taken a sequence of dialogue and cut it enormously – taken out half of it. Then I look at it and I take out more. I keep taking chunks away. I think this is legitimate but I am worried because it is tampering. But at the same time I think the verbal side of it, from a stage point of view, has a kind of function that on film is not necessary. . . . I'm not rewriting Shakespeare. I'm making a film.'

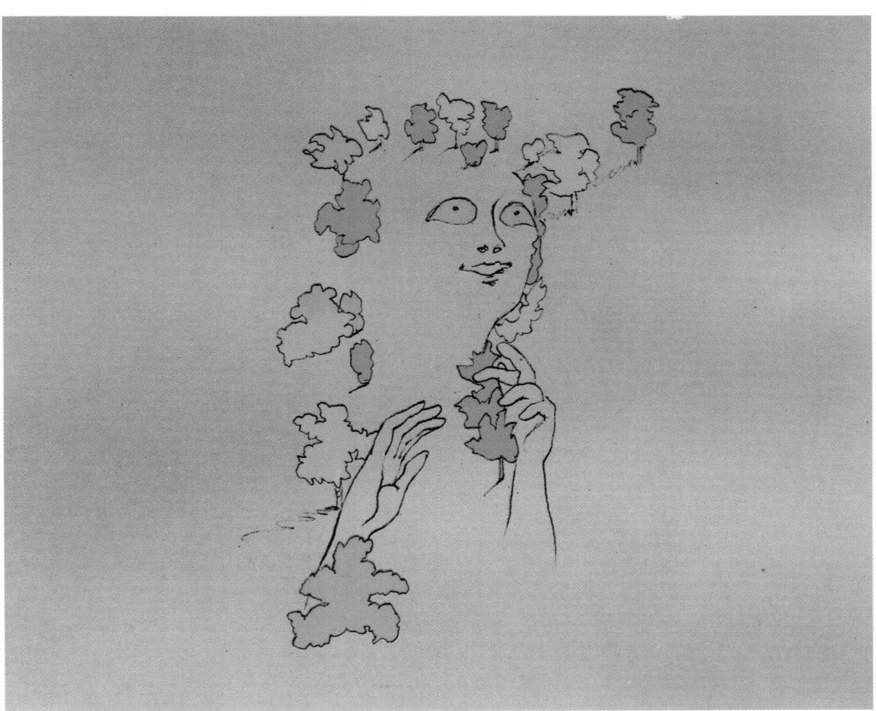

Opposite page, above left: *The Flying Man* (1962); left: *Yellow Submarine* (1968); far left: television commercial for Golden Wonder Crisps (1960); above: the Beatles, as depicted in *Yellow Submarine* (1968); right: two of the drawings from the unfinished film *The Tempest*

HALAS AND BATCHELOR

The Halas and Batchelor studio was formed by myself and Joy Batchelor in 1940 and during its long period of activity produced some 2000 shorts and seven feature-length animated films. We discovered early on that flexibility and adaptability were essential in order to survive the difficult periods in the film industry (which occur every five years or so in Britain) and the changes in trends, fashions and tastes of both clients and public. The market in Britain is very small in comparison with that in America, which means that it is far more difficult here to create a popular, identifiable character along the lines of Mickey, Donald or Popeye as well as maintaining the momentum of a studio. Nevertheless, if we did not succeed in creating an 'immortal' character, we were able to create certain trends in animation and invent a number of new systems.

I was born in Budapest, Hungary, in 1912 and came to England in 1936, after a period of extensive study in graphic design with Alexander Bortnyik and Moholy-Nagy, both former tutors at the Bauhaus. Joy Batchelor was born in 1914 in Watford, North London, and was a pupil at the local Art College. After joining up as a graphic design team at the beginning of the war we were asked by the J. Walter Thompson agency to make long advertising cartoons for some of their clients, such as Kelloggs, Lux and Rinso. The Ministry of Information came across our work and virtually commanded us to produce informational and propaganda films for the remainder of the war.

This involvement in producing films aimed at general audiences (war information films and educational and promotional films for companies like BP, Shell and Esso) may have been responsible for furthering the wider acceptance of adult cartoons. We also aimed the *Poet and Painter* series at an adult audience. This was made for the celebratory Festival of Britain in 1951 and featured specially commissioned work from several outstanding artists, including Henry Moore, Michael Rothenstein and Mervyn Peake. The following year we made the experimental stereoscopic film *The Owl and the Pussycat* based on Edward Lear's Victorian nonsense poem. It was seven minutes long and was Europe's first three-dimensional film.

Another experimental work was the puppet film *The Figurehead* (1953), using Crosbie Garstin's poem about a lovesick mermaid and original music by Matyas Seiber. The animation was done after the music was composed and was carefully synchronised with the musical rhythm and structure. Our animated version of George Orwell's *Animal Farm* was released in 1954 and was the first animated feature-length film made in Britain (see page 34). One of our most difficult assignments came in 1953. We were asked to act as art directors for the feature *Cinerama Holiday* and to animate the bridging sections between episodes of this gigantic feature which stretched across the screen at 142 degrees.

Another innovation, the film *Ruddigore* (directed by Joy Batchelor in 1964), was the first cartoon opera, adapted from Gilbert and Sullivan's original.

Right: *Animal Farm* (1954); below: *The Tales of Hoffnung* (1964); below right: *Dilemma* (1981); below far right: from *Leonardo da Vinci* (designed by Janos Kass) in the *Great Masters* series (1985); opposite page: *Ruddigore* (1964)

The studio, under its training scheme headed by Harold Whitaker (a key animator of outstanding technical skill), trained a number of animators who today have leading positions in the animation industry.

From the mid-sixties onwards the Halas and Batchelor studio made a number of self-financed shorts like *Automania 2000* (1963), *The Question* (1967) and *The Cultured Ape* (1962). I produced and directed a series for BBC TV based on Gerard Hoffnung's drawings, *The Tales of Hoffnung* (1964), which was followed by several hundred television films for the USA.

In the mid-seventies, Joy Batchelor retired from active production. I continued to make a number of experimental films using the new technique of computer animation such as *Autobahn* in 1979 and *Dilemma* in 1981. I then went on to direct and produce a series of films about the lives of the great masters of art such as Leonardo da Vinci, Michelangelo, Botticelli, Toulouse-Lautrec and Hieronymus Bosch, again using computer animation.

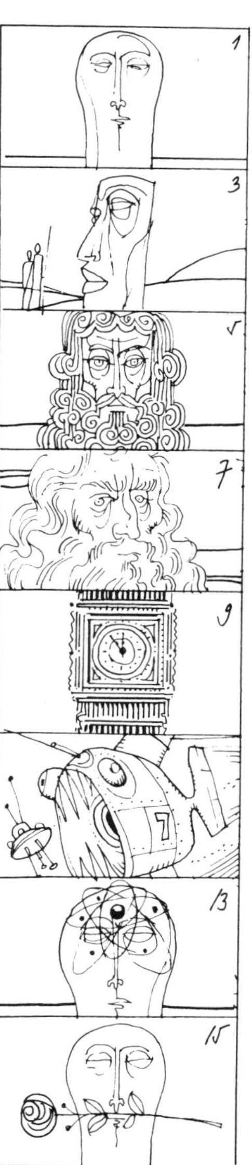

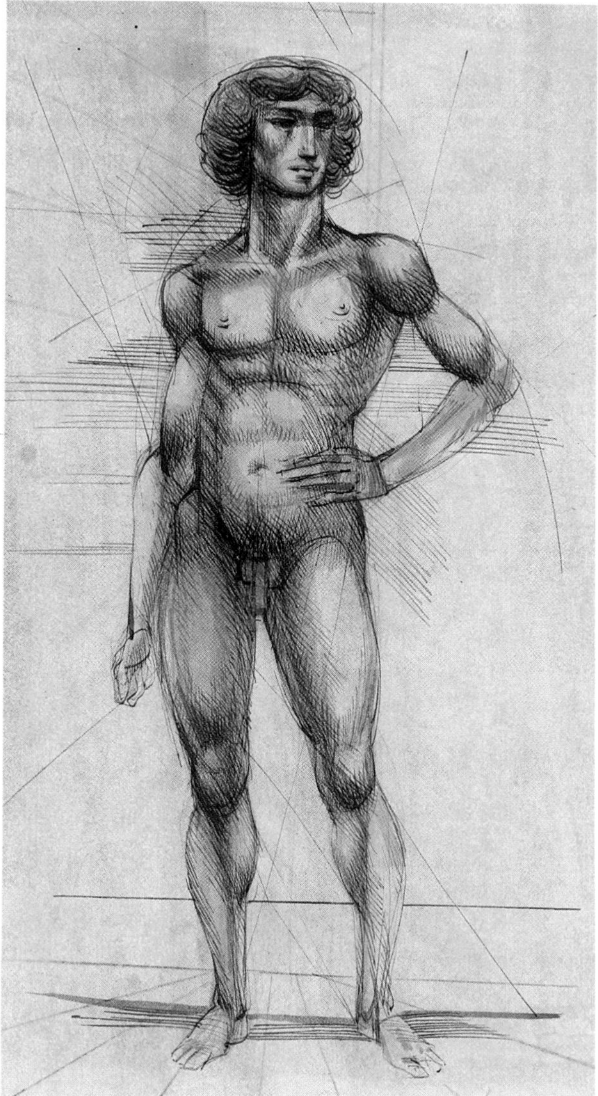

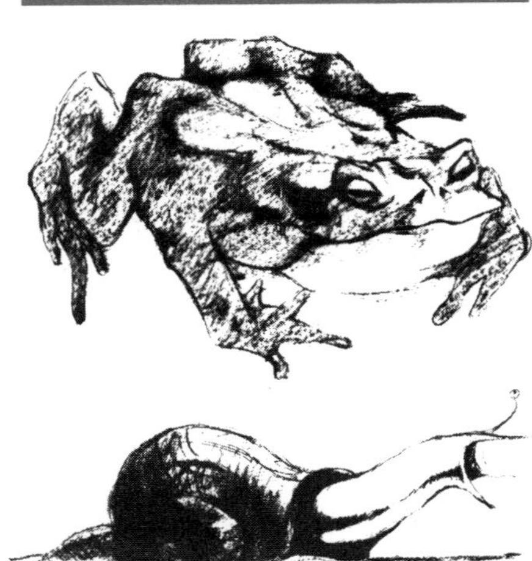

Below: *Ubu* (1979); below left and above: three drawings from *Lautrec* (1975); above left: *Tomfoolery* (1971)

Geoff Dunbar's strength as an animator lies primarily in the originality of his design. He has a natural, artistic talent and his graphics would succeed just as well in static print as in moving pictures. He is able to convey the inner essence of characters while still retaining some surface aspects, using both to great effect.

He was born in Oxfordshire in 1944 and began work at the W. M. Larkins studio in London. Three years later he joined us at Halas and Batchelor, contributing his talents to several award-winning animated commercials. He then went on to form Dragon Productions with some colleagues, and it was during this period that he produced and directed the short film *Lautrec* (1975) based on the cancan drawings of the French artist. The film won the Palm d'Or at the Cannes Film Festival and a Silver award at the New York Film Festival.

Possibly the most interesting of his films, however, is *Ubu* (1979), based on Alfred Jarry's stage play *Ubu Roi*, an experimental piece of theatre first performed in 1896. Jarry had originally intended his play to be for the Chinese shadow puppet theatre and Dunbar decided that it would translate well into animated form, especially as its strongly defined characters suited his own 'grotesque' style. The Arts Council of Great Britain put up half the finance and *Ubu* became a twenty-minute film containing a bold visual design which shocked the critics and (even more so) the distributors. The film was awarded prizes at many international festivals, notably the Golden Bear at the Berlin Film Festival, in 1980. The film expresses a great deal of anger, and its dynamic confrontations open the way to original graphic forms. One of his most recent films is *Rupert and the Frog Song* (based on the famous *Daily Express* cartoon strip Rupert the Bear), which he made in collaboration with Paul McCartney. The film won a 1985 British Academy Award.

RAOUL SERVAIS

Raoul Servais's films synthesise some of the best elements in Flemish culture. His stories are fundamentally humane and full of pathos and they highlight the dramatic confrontations between different aspects of human nature. His designs are original, assured and expressive; his techniques search to apply new solutions to the problems presented, and his film craftsmanship is competent and professional.

He was born in Ostend, Belgium, in 1928 and studied art at the Royal Academy of Art in Ghent. Even as a young amateur film-maker he was interested in the potential of animated film. At an early age he experimented with a Pathe-baby camera following the visual treatment found in Chaplin's pantomime and Pat Sullivan's Felix the Cat. His first real attempt was made with his treasured 9.5mm camera in 1946, a film entitled *A Ghost Story*. Although it is primitive he claims to have learnt an enormous amount from his mistakes.

In 1952 he assisted the distinguished Belgian painter René Magritte in the making of the mural painting *L'Empire du Rêve*.

His film titles since the early 1960s read as a roll of honour. *The False Note* (1963) is the moral tale of a beggar and a comment on human stupidity, while *Chromophobia* (1966) is a highly imaginative story which stands up for freedom of spirit. *Sirène* (1968) is a delightful film about a mermaid, an amorous cabin boy and a solitary fisherman; when the mermaid suddenly comes to life she brings hope and freedom. In 1969 he made *Goldframe*, which is about an indulgent film-maker who gets his just deserts.

In the seventies, Servais went on to make the film *To Speak or Not to Speak* (1970), a moral tale about totalitarian power, and *Operation X-70* (1971), about the exploitation of power with the invention of the new gas X-70. Original etching was tried out as background for this film. *Pegasus* (1973) was a dramatic tale about a farrier's dream-world being invaded by thousands of horses. The visuals were inspired by the expressionist school of Flemish painting at the beginning of this century.

Servais's most unique film, however, is *Harpya* (1979). Its originality partly lies in its ability to tell the old story of the mythological character of the blood-sucking harpy with a fresh approach, but also in the introduction of a novel technique. The film is a combination of live-action and plastic stop-motion shooting and the two levels are controlled perfectly to achieve a fully integrated composite image. The film won the Palm d'Or at Cannes in 1979.

For the Belgian cinema and for European animation, Servais represents an original talent and as a professor of animated art in the Academy of Arts in Ghent he is considered to be a brilliant teacher.

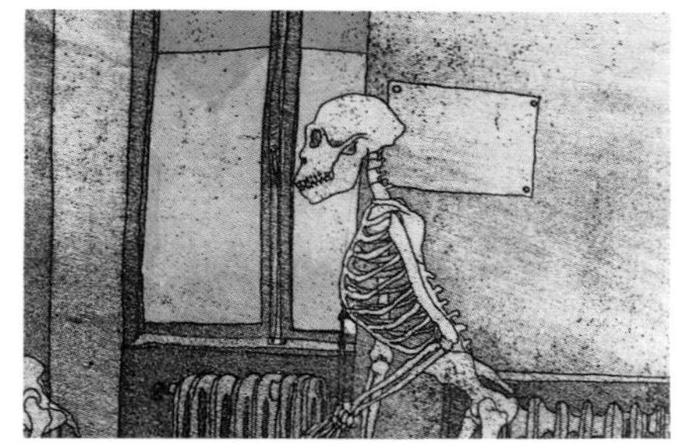

Above left: *Goldframe* (1969); left: *Operation X-70* (1971); below: *Harpya* (1979)

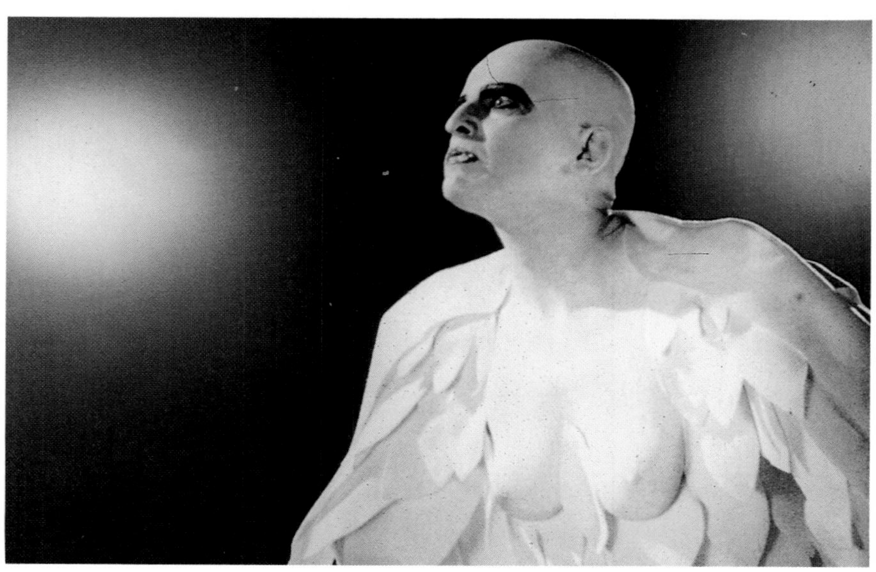

MARCELL JANKOVICS

Marcell Jankovics is possibly the most well-known representative of Hungarian animation. Apart from his own films, both long and short, he has contributed to the production of many films made by other directors at the Pannonia Studios and the credit for directing the very first Hungarian feature-length animated film, *John the Hero* (1973), goes to Jankovics.

He was born in Budapest, Hungary, in 1941 and joined the Pannonia Film at an early age in 1960. His first contribution was the television series *Gusztav*, which featured a character symbolising a typical Hungarian citizen: he designed the model of the figure and directed many of the episodes. Through the series, which was primarily aimed at an adult audience, he gained enough confidence to start a series of highly independent productions, some with interesting psychological implications. The most successful were *Deep Water* (1970), *Sisyphus* (1974) and *The Fight* (1977). Most of them achieved international recognition and top awards at international festivals.

Above: two drawings from *Sisyphus* (1974); right: *The Fight* (1977); opposite page, top: *John the Hero* (1973); bottom: a scene from *Hungarian Folk-Tales* (1977)

His feature *John the Hero* is based on the work of the nationally acclaimed poet Petöfi (1823–49) and is a romantic tale of a handsome soldier and his adventures in the land of the fairies. The introduction of folk-art as a motif throughout the film gave the feature added colour and a touch of visual originality which also seems to run through most of his other work, like his successful feature *Son of the White Mare* (1981). This is also based on an old Hungarian folk-tale, and it gave him plenty of scope for spectacle and clever transformations which caught (and kept) the audience's interest.

He has given inspiration and provided technical competence to the series *Hungarian Folk-Tales* (1977), which is still being made for television in Pannonia's other studio at Kecskemét. In order to retain the original flavour of these traditional folk-tales, Jankovics carried out detailed research into archives and interviewed many villagers. In spite of their quantity, the quality of these films is way above the normal run of factory-type television animated films. He is much appreciated both at home, where he has received the highly coveted Kossuth Prize, and outside his country, where he has served on many international film festival juries.

ATTILA DARGAY

Dargay seems to be a natural entertainer whose top priority is to achieve as close a contact with his audiences as possible. He has no difficulty in succeeding with this since he is a very appealing artist whose work is easy on the eye and uncomplicated in content. This makes him probably the most popular film-cartoonist in Hungary. He is especially liked by the younger generation, who are able to recognise his cartoon figures as real characters and are able to identify closely with them.

He was born in 1927, in the small country town of Mezötúr, Hungary, and is one of the longest-standing workers in Pannonia Film. His early period was spent understudying Gyula Macskassy, one of the original pioneers of Hungarian animation. Macskassy's influence was an excellent guideline in learning how to capture audience attention and how to simplify animated figures to get the maximum number of facial expressions out of them. Dargay greatly benefited by this and became a highly professional animator and a creator of totally fluid cartoon characterisation, which is an art only a few can acquire.

After a number of amusing short films his major chance arose with the feature film *Ludas Matyi* (*The Goose Boy*) in 1976. The story followed a traditional old Hungarian folk-tale, but Dargay's interpretation was witty, the characters amusing, and he injected enough original ideas to make the film a popular success.

His next feature's success even exceeded his first. *Vuk* (*The Fox*), released in 1981, was another film which charmed popular audiences. The subject of the film, the cunning fox pitted against man and being outmanoeuvred, has huge audience appeal and Dargay's treatment cleverly exploited the sympathy which was inherent in the subject.

His latest feature *Szaffi* (1984) is a romantic tale from the seventeenth century, and is a story of an inheritance from father to son. There are some interesting animal figures woven into the story to offset the drama unfolding among the humans.

Dargay is a great asset to the field of Hungarian animation. His work continually asserts the fundamental value of full animation. His films, always informed by the skill of the true draughtsman, are loved by adults and children alike.

Left: *Ludas Matyi* (1976); below: *Szaffi* (1984); below left: *Vuk* (1981)

JOSEF NEPP

Josef Nepp is perhaps the most versatile member of the Hungarian animated film industry. He is able to perform a variety of functions: from being an 'ideas man', to drawing storyboards; creating characters; animating; producing; directing; even composing his own music and playing instruments. Such versatility is indeed useful in a studio where the output is high and new people often enter production with insufficient experience.

He was born in Csepel, a small industrial town near Budapest, Hungary, in 1934. He studied at the Academy of Industrial Artists, after which he was soon offered a position at the Pannonia Film in Budapest, where he still works. Nepp started as a background painter, but soon graduated to making publicity films for local clients and had an opportunity to work with the talented Hungarian animator, Gyula Macskassy and later with Dargay and Jankovics, learning how to achieve an effect by the simplest lines and graphic shapes. His own true speciality is irony and with penetrating wit he exploits his black humour to the extreme. His 1966 film *Five Minutes of Murder*, for instance, consists of 150 different murderous situations. Audiences never know whether to laugh or be shocked, but they are usually amused by the fluidity of the sequences and 'enjoy' the horrific experience.

In 1983 he made *Snow White*. His feature did not have much to do with the Brothers Grimm and had little in common with the Disney version. This long film turned out to be an analysis of criminology with ironical observations, but also had enough humour and entertainment content to survive.

Since 1968 he has been teaching animation at his old college, the Academy of Industrial Artists. Among his numerous awards are several from the State including one which is entitled Excellent Artist, and after nearly thirty years of consistently good creative activity, he certainly deserves them all.

Above: *Bang Tititi* (1967); below: *Snow White* (1983); below right, top: *Five Minutes of Murder* (1966); below right, bottom: *Gusztav* (1976)

BRUNO BOZZETTO

Bruno Bozzetto has achieved an international reputation through his consistency of output, his inimitable style of grotesque characters, and his highly individual sense of caricature. He can define with the simplest of outlines the essence of a personality which is instantly recognisable and appealing.

He was born in Milan, Italy, in 1938. His early education consisted of classical studies and some years at university devoted to Law and Geology. He entered animation and design at the age of seventeen and his excellent film, *Tapum*, was shown at the Cannes International Film Festival in 1958 when he was only twenty. Its humour, design and timing revealed a fresh approach to film-making and persuaded me to invite him to study the craft of animation at the Halas and Batchelor studio in London, which he did for one year.

As a film cartoonist he is able to develop his characters with the right behaviour patterns and to create a rounded personality for them. One of his stock characters, Il Signor Rossi, who appeared in numerous short cartoons from 1960 onwards and in three of his feature-length films, became the symbol of the Italian 'little man'; resourceful, determined, greedy and vain but with a great deal of charm, who puts his family interests above all others.

Bozzetto's rare asset is his ability to co-ordinate and control so many disparate elements: story continuity and development; characterisation of personalities; complementary sound effects and music (which underline the behaviour of his figures); humour (which never steps out of context) and ideas (which are always within the bounds of the technical flexibility of animation). His sharp European wit differs from American humour (which is usually more physical), inasmuch as it contains a satirical comment on human shortcomings like greed and stupidity. Nevertheless his humour is light; it is never didactic and retains the strong Italian tradition of commedia dell'arté.

His large output includes several series for television and six full-length animated feature films. He reached a high point with *Allegro non Troppo* in 1976; a parody of a grand symphony concert and the unexpected happenings which could occur during such a concert. The film combines a very pleasing quality of graphic design, close relationships between choreography and music and a strong sense of visual progression. Several of his shorter films such as *Alpha-Omega* (1961), *Ego* (1969), *Opera* (1972) and *Self-Service* (1974) have become classic cautionary tales for our time and are examples of the integration of graphic design, storytelling and subtle humour.

Today Bruno Bozzetto is considered one of the outstanding creators of satirical and humorous animation, and one who can combine the traditional Italian comic style with modern graphics.

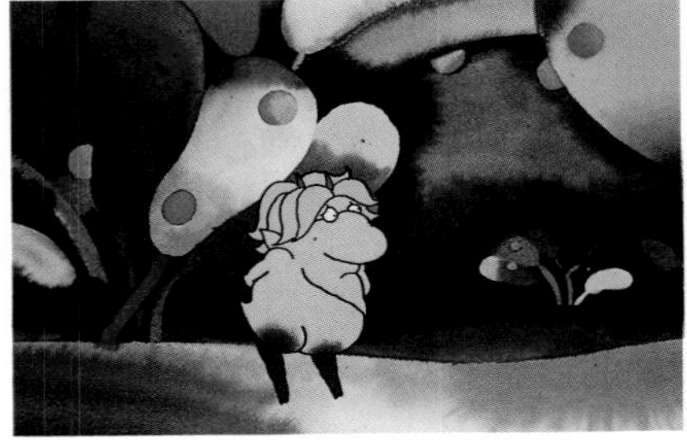

Left: *Un Oscar por Il Signor Rossi* (1960); above and top: *Allegro non Troppo* (1976); opposite page, top: *Allegro non Troppo;* bottom: *My Superman Brother VIP* (1968)

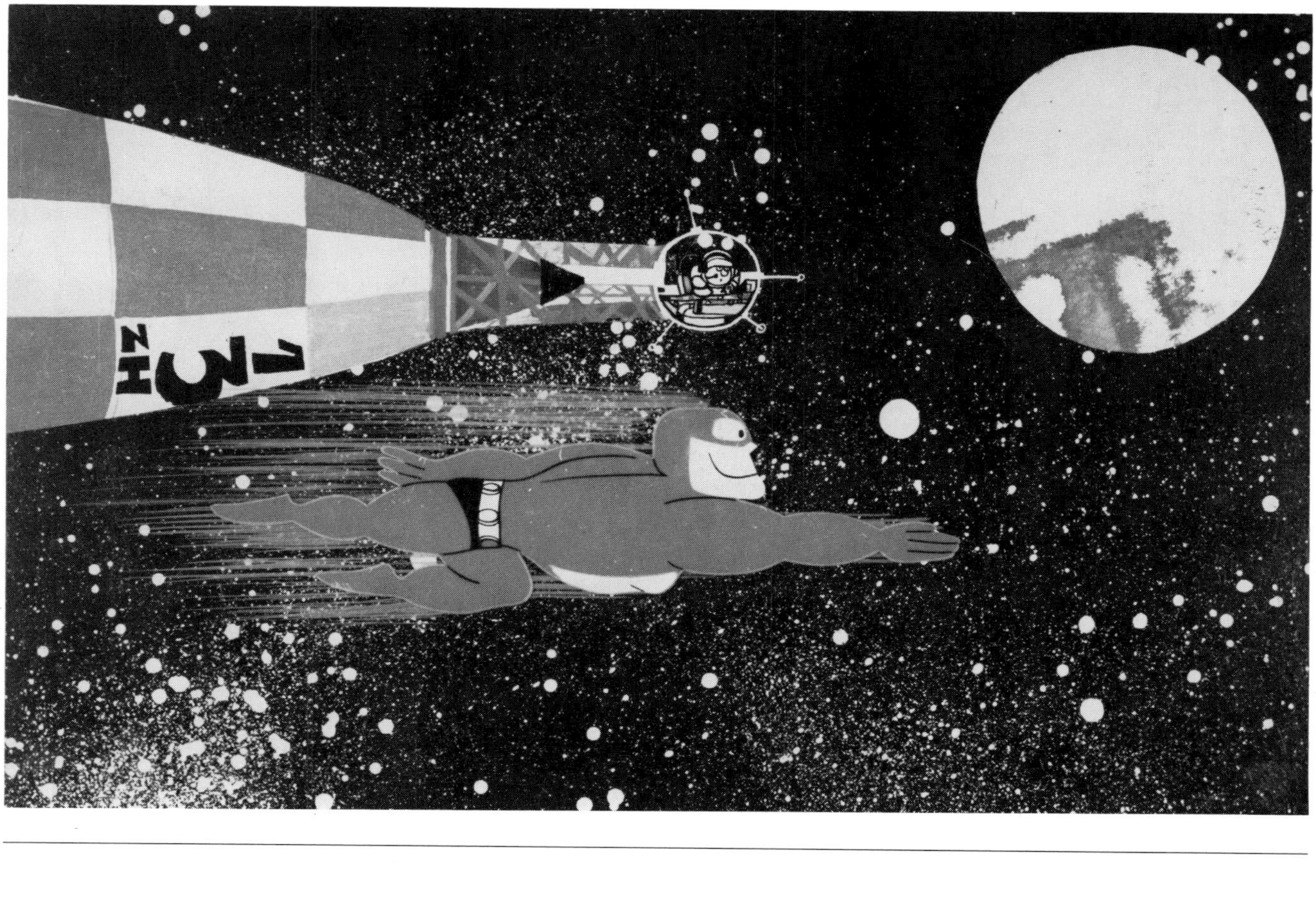

LUZZATI AND GIANINI

Emanuele Luzzati, animated film director and scenic designer for the theatre, was born in Genoa, Italy, in 1921. A graduate of the Ecole des Beaux Arts in Lausanne and a highly accomplished painter, decorator, illustrator and ceramicist, he began his career in stage and costume design and expanded his work to include film-making and animation. He has since collaborated with Giulio Gianini (born in Rome in 1927) in the production of many animated films, including *The Paladins of France* (1960), *Ali Baba* (1971), the Academy Award nomination *Pulcinella* (1973) and *Turandot* (1974).

Luzzati is almost unique in being able to pursue two careers at the same time: stage design for opera, ballet and the theatre and animated film for the cinema and television. His rich talent has many facets and he has his own distinctive style which is successfully shown in his animated film characters. They are light, humorous figures, with bold simple lines, and their shapes allow them to be expanded easily into movement, which is carried out by Gianini.

Their co-operation in the medium of film animation dates back to 1957, with Gianini animating Luzzati's figures and photographing them under the rostrum camera. Luzzati drew the characters and designed the backgrounds and together they worked on the story development and timing of the action. They both chose the music and fitted the story to it later.

Both men know how to exploit space with clever choreography, using entirely different skills. Luzzati's stage work for the European theatre is outstanding. He has designed sets and costumes for La Scala, Milan, and for opera houses in Rome, Naples, Venice, Florence and Genoa. He has worked for the London Festival Ballet, for Glyndebourne and designed costumes for *Così fan tutte* and *The Magic Flute*. Gianini, on the other hand, is basically a film animator, concentrating on motion and the mechanics of movement. His visual effects are always tailored to the potential of the camera. Using pre-programmed movements for the backgrounds, he organises his cut-out figures in a highly imaginative way.

The two artists are well co-ordinated, each contributing his own talents which complement the other perfectly. In contrast to Luzzati, whose work is broad and general, Gianini's is technical and exact in detail. Luzzati's style is colourful and decorative, and he has a strong personality when it comes to pictorial invention. His film designs contain a great deal of pictorial beauty and a sense of optimism and humour which counterbalances some of the self-consciousness of the music on which most of their subjects are based.

The work of Luzzati and Gianini is typified by their distinctive style of synchronising the visuals and the music. This sense emerges most strongly in their film of Mozart's last opera *The Magic Flute* (1977), their longest production so far. The choreography of the animation follows the rhythm of the music and is able to interpret it with all its delicacy and subtlety. This interpretation of music is one of their assets and it is very much in the foreground in their other films which utilise Rossini's scores such as *The Thieving Magpie* (1964) and *An Italian Girl in Algiers* (1968).

Below: *The Magic Flute* (1977); opposite page: *Turandot* (1974)

MANFREDO MANFREDI

Manfredo Manfredi's style perhaps owes more to the tradition of classical Italian art than to the work of his contemporaries. His craftsmanship is unique. As opposed to Luzzati (see page 92), whose figures are composed of graphic shapes, Manfredi's figures are solid constructions built on three-dimensional spheres. They contain a classical and sensual harmony of form, and his stories deal with one of humanity's most fundamental conflicts: the struggle between good and evil. His presentations bring to mind the great Italian dramas.

He was born in Palermo, Italy, in 1934, and is a graduate of film art at the Accademia di Belle Arti in Rome, finishing there in 1958. His apprenticeship was spent assisting as a junior in theatrical, and later in cinema and television, productions. He eventually became a director of animated film in 1965, working in collaboration with Guido Gomas. In 1974, after directing a number of distinguished short films, he directed *L'Uva Salamanna* in the series *European Folk-Tales*, applying his elegant classical Italian style of design to convey a traditional local folk-tale. It is the story of a wedding in Tuscany and uses traditional Renaissance imagery, reminiscent of Mantegna's visual approach, providing an atmosphere of pathos, despair and beauty. The *European Folk-Tales* project was supported by another outstanding artist, Maximillian Massimo Garnier, who later produced *Dedalo* (*The Labyrinth*) in 1977 with Manfredi's direction. The full flavour of Manfredi's skill, both as a film-maker and designer, came to light with this film. In it he rises above the documentary aspect of the story and brings depth, visual invention, surrealism and an exciting dynamic to the treatments. *Dedalo* is a typical Manfredi film. He drew every single drawing himself (there were 14,000), taking over a year to finish the film. *Dedalo* demonstrates Manfredi's skill, patience, energy and instinct for film continuity. This film was nominated for an Oscar and was first prize-winner in the Ottawa Festival.

Among his latest works are two notable title designs for television programmes: *Total Shakespeare* (1974) and *The Genius of the Cinema: Orson Welles* (1984). Both are distinguished by the quality of their design and imaginative, entertaining approach. Manfredi now works in Rome with Aldo Raparelli and Max Garnier at Cineteam, helping to ensure that the output of the unit remains among the best in Italy.

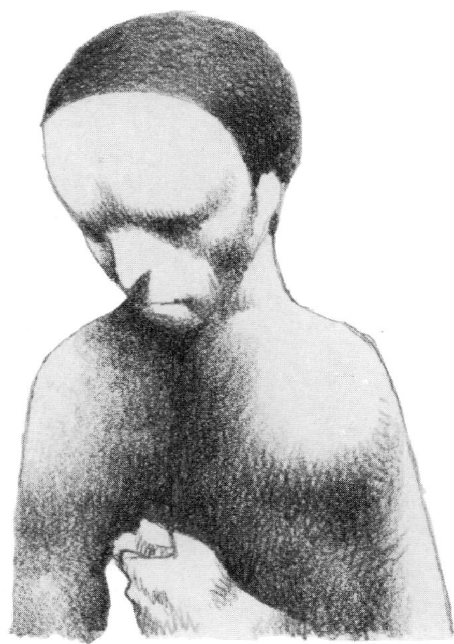

Left and bottom: *Dedalo* (1977); below: *The Genius of the Cinema: Orson Welles* (1984)

PAUL GRIMAULT

Paul Grimault's fifty years of artistic activity covers almost the whole period of French animation. He was fortunate to be associated, in his early days, with such outstanding artists as the film-maker Marcel Carné, the painter Max Ernst and the famous French comedian Jacques Tati.

Grimault was born in 1905 in Neuilly-sur-Seine, near Paris. He was trained as a graphic designer and in his early professional period he joined an advertising agency and was responsible for many short publicity films. He soon emerged as a strong force in the glorious tradition of French animation, represented by Emile Cohl and, previously, by the magical cinematography of Georges Méliès. He was certainly the most outstanding representative of the early period of French animation and was responsible for a new approach with a new look. This style had a much richer visual content and was nearer to the quality of graphical fine art than a caricatured comic strip. This school of French animation was established immediately after the Second World War with such films as *Le Voleur de Paratonnerres* in 1945, *La Flûte Magique* in 1946, and a charming short film in 1947, *Le Petit Soldat*.

In 1958, after doing a number of commercial films, he did *La Faim du Monde*; in 1969, *Le Diamant* and in 1973, *Le Chien Mélomane*, a philosophical short film about a subject tackled by so many contemporary animators: the atomic bomb. By this time his style was firmly established and was taken up by a new generation of young French artists, Jean-François Laguionie, Jacques Colombat and Emil Bourget. In their visual style they closely follow Grimault's classicism and rich visual treatment of backgrounds.

Grimault's most notable achievement was the feature film *The King and Mr Bird* which he finally completed in 1979. It was an instant success and he received a major national prize for it (see page 32). After some fifty years of intense work, Paul Grimault is still active and planning his next feature film.

Above right: *Le Chien Mélomane* (1973); right: *The King and Mr Bird* (1979)

ALEXANDRE ALEXEIEFF AND CLAIRE PARKER

Among professional film-makers and film critics, the names of Alexandre Alexeieff and Claire Parker are synonymous with the poetry of moving images. They both started as painters, but like so many other fine artists were excited by the prospect of making their paintings move in time and space. After this development, Alexeieff declared (in Paris, where he settled in 1921) that French easel painting was dead: he was devoting his attention to the work of the upcoming masters. The mood was then to concentrate on composition and texture and he subsequently became preoccupied with exhaustive experiments in engraving.

It was in the late twenties that Alexeieff (Russian by birth) met Claire Parker, a talented American art student living in Paris. They joined forces and together built the pin screen, a device which enabled them to animate Alexeieff's engravings. In 1933 they conceived their first film, *Animated Engravings*, with the aid of this invention, and for the first time an image could remain composed in spite of its movement.

The pin screen apparatus consists of a 1m × 1.2m white plate, held upright in a frame allowing access to both front and rear surfaces. It accommodates a million steel rods which can be pushed freely to a determined position with small rollers; various tones are obtainable according to the position of the rods. The method provides for the most refined engraving techniques possible, is well suited to lyrical works and gives the artist complete autonomy. Its texture is similar to that of the half-tone print and provides shading, unlike normal animated cartoon techniques.

Their first film made entirely with the pin screen, *Night on Bare Mountain* in 1933 (based on Mussorgsky's music), opened up new horizons in animated art. Fine art had at last been successfully fused with the art of animation.

But the experiment, while a great success with professionals, was not a hit with film distributors. The film ran for six weeks at the Panthéon in Paris and for only two weeks at the Academy in London. Nevertheless, they pressed forward and produced a great number of highly original advertising films, enabling them to survive while improving the structure of the pin screen.

During the war they established themselves in Canada, where they continued to develop their apparatus at the National Film Board. The second pin screen was bigger and more sophisticated with 1,400,000 rods. They made the film *En Passant* (1943) with this new machine.

Back in Europe they made a number of memorable films, some based on classical Russian subjects: *Earth Juices* (1955), *The Disguised* and *Pure Beauty* (1956), and *The Nose* (1963), based on Gogol's story about a man who lost his nose, with music by Hai Minh. Later they released *Pictures at an Exhibition* in 1972 and *Three Themes* in 1977, both based on Mussorgsky's musical scores.

Alexeieff and Parker were very much aware that their system of work was painstakingly slow. Each frame could take hours to set and a short film of eight minutes could take a year and a half to produce. But no matter: after forty-five years of practice they believed that the process of motion picture animation is an acceleration of images and events entirely created by the impression of the artist. They felt that by leaving the three-dimensional world of humanity behind they entered into the fourth dimension and that animation's destiny is to take the place of painting. Easel painting, they claimed, was lost in a maze of sterile, scholastic polemics and speculation: the future would show what animation could do.

JEAN-FRANÇOIS LAGUIONIE

Jean-François Laguionie's predilection for injecting pathos and drama into his narratives makes his work closer to the East European tradition of animation than the more typically American approach, which aims for the purest possible visual form in order to maximise the effect of the burlesque gags. Like many of his European colleagues, Laguionie has a strong personal style and richly sculpted and textured characters and backgrounds.

He was born in Besançon, France, in 1939, and studied art at the School of Applied Arts in Paris. The Chinese Puppet Theatre there made a strong impression on him and that influence is still evident in his work today.

Laguionie's work was originally noticed when his first film, *La Demoiselle et le Violoncelliste* (*The Girl and the Cellist*), won the Annecy Grand Prix in 1965. The originality of his design and the understated humour of the film immediately attracted attention. His subsequent films, *Noah's Ark* (1965) and *A Bomb By Accident* (1968), were given instant recognition with awards from other festivals in Poland, Romania and in France.

After a series of further productions in collaboration with his wife Kali Carlini (a highly talented painter), he received the Palm d'Or for short films in the 1978 Cannes International Film Festival with *La Traversée de l'Atlantique à la Rame* (*Rowing Across the Atlantic*).

Laguionie designs and makes his metallic cut-outs with astonishing skill and dexterity. He manipulates them under the camera personally, knowing precisely the nature of their characters and their behaviour patterns. His latest work is his first feature-length film, entitled *Le Livre de Sable* (1985), the British title of which is *Gwen*. It is quite an achievement, as he created and photographed every single frame of the long film (which lasts eighty minutes) on his own. He finds that in this way he can be in complete command of the medium and produce an undiluted expression of his ideas.

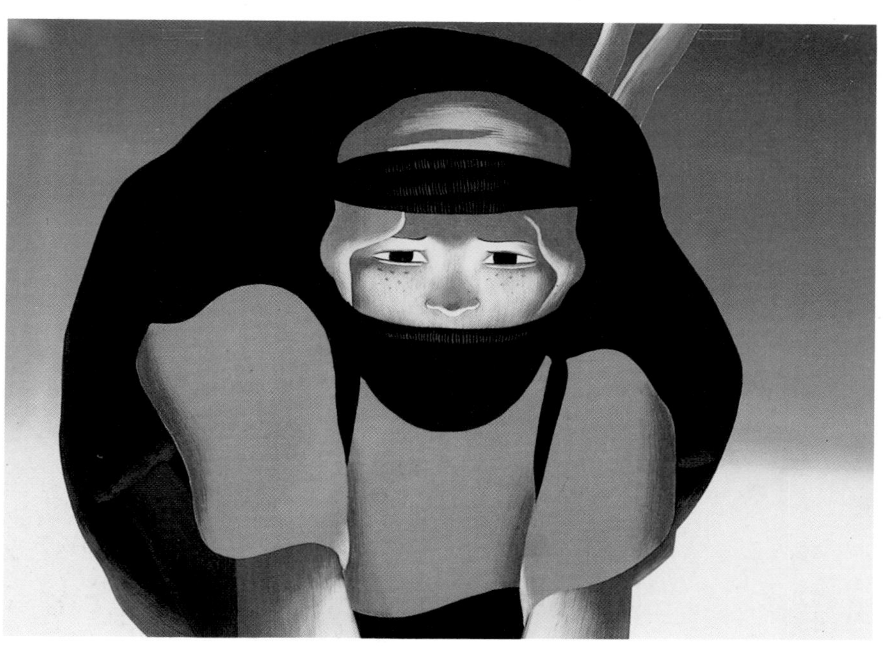

Above right: *La Traversée de L'Atlantique à la Rame* (1978); right: *Le Livre de Sable* or *Gwen* (1985); opposite page: Alexeieff and Parker's *En Passant* (1943)

KAREL ZEMAN

Karel Zeman is a master of puppetry, fantasy and film craft. During his lifetime he has received the highest international honours and awards, although the title he most appreciates, he says, is National Artist of Czechoslovakia.

Zeman was born in 1910 in Moravia, Czechoslovakia, and was trained as a designer. He was one of the co-founders of the Gottwaldov Film Studio in 1943. He used materials which other animators avoided at all costs: since glass was plentiful in Czechoslovakia, he decided to prove that a great deal could be done with it. In spite of its hard, unyielding qualities he successfully animated it with the aid of a glass-blower and created the film *Inspiration* in 1949.

In 1947 he created the popular character Mr Prokouk, a symbol of bureaucracy; through the production of a cinema series this character became a national hero and these films continued to be made until 1959.

He made his first long film, *Journey into Prehistory*, in 1955 and invented a number of prehistoric characters which he handled with skill and a great deal of humour. In *The Invention of Destruction*, another long film made in 1958, he warned the world of its possible destruction as a result of its lethal inventions. He explored the special effects potential of the subject as well as its graphic possibilities; at that time these effects were extremely difficult to

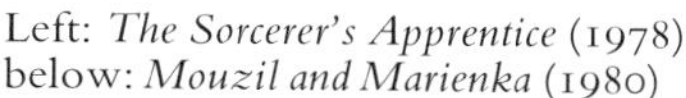

Left: *The Sorcerer's Apprentice* (1978); below: *Mouzil and Marienka* (1980)

obtain and could only be achieved with special processes.

He continued to explore the large-scale aspects of the cinema screen with further long films full of imagination and fantasy. *Baron Munchhausen* (1961) was a combination of live-action photography and animated etchings, which gave the film a textured, nineteenth-century look. *On the Comet* (1969) was from the novel by Jules Verne, Zeman's favourite supplier of stories who provides him with plenty of adventures, entertainment and dramatic fiction.

Zeman's contact with children is through popular classics like *A Jester's Tale* (1964), *The Adventures of Sinbad the Sailor* (1971) and *The Sorcerer's Apprentice* (1978). His stories always feature a villain and a hero and he is a master of how to manipulate a situation in order to involve his audience to the full. He is primarily an entertainer with great originality and cinematographic skill: he is only secondarily a moralist and is never a dull teacher.

Below: *Treasure of Bird Island* (1952); opposite page: *The Invention of Destruction* (1958)

JIRI TRNKA

Jiri Trnka was a film-maker who became a legend in his own lifetime. He was not only a true master of the craft of puppetry but was able to enrich his characters in three dimensions through the medium of motion pictures.

Trnka was born in Pisek, Czechoslovakia, in 1912. A graduate of the Prague School of Arts and Crafts, he was trained as a sculptor and painter and later studied graphics and lithography. He gravitated towards the theatre, becoming an apprentice to the puppet-master Josef Skupa, who had a significant influence upon him.

His main contribution, apart from his influence in the visual arts, was in the area of story-telling. In that capacity he was equal to the writer Lewis Carroll, expressing himself in the form of pictures and puppets instead of words. After the Second World War, the strength of his reputation increased throughout Europe. The medium of the Czech language, of course, could not have crossed the borders into the rest of Europe, but his powerful characters were easily assimilated and understood. His subtle, restrained humour, his ardent patriotism and longing for justice appealed to the post-war international public just emerging from the gloom and depression of the war years.

His success at home, however, was not immediate. His critics found it difficult to accept comedy, drama and tragedy portrayed by moving puppets. Before he was fully recognised at home he had to have success outside Czechoslovakia, which he achieved with the feature-length puppet film *The Emperor's Nightingale* in 1948, *Prince Bayaya* in 1950 and *The Old Czech Legend* in 1953. These convinced the nation that he was indeed an outstanding artist.

When he made *A Midsummer Night's Dream* in 1959, he was accused of being over-confident in attempting to tackle Shakespearian poetry, the subtleness of characterisation associated with the play and the theatrical spectacle. It was felt that he succeeded with the latter but fell short in the two former categories.

His real strength emerged in subjects like *The Good Soldier Schweik* series (1954), where he could parody the pomposity of the establishment and emphasise the defiance of the main character. In his short film *The Hand* (1965) he made an imaginative plea for the freedom of a creative artist who defied authority by doing what he wanted instead of producing propaganda. The central character, the sculptor carving a warning hand out of the stone, could be easily identified with Trnka and the things he stood for throughout his life.

Below: *A Midsummer Night's Dream* (1959); opposite page, top: *The Good Soldier Schweik* (1954); bottom: *The Hand* (1965)

BRETISLAV POJAR

Bretislav Pojar is a true disciple of the great puppet-master Jiri Trnka and the Czech school of puppet animation. As a versatile artist in his own right he has directed a number of films using normal cel animation methods, mainly for the United Nations and the National Film Board of Canada. He has also developed a system half-way between the two methods using plastic puppets which are photographed in semi-relief. This method has produced some new and unusual effects not attempted before by any other animator.

Bretislav Pojar was born in Susice, Czechoslovakia, in 1923. He started as an assistant animator with Jiri Brdecka and Stanislav Latal when he was only nineteen. He eventually became Trnka's best animator working on his film *The Emperor's Nightingale* (1948). Pojar's technical competence in puppetry and his understanding of its complex techniques is undoubtedly due to this period of training and his close contact with Trnka.

In 1954 he began to direct his own films. With his new-found independence he was soon able to demonstrate his creative talents and was made head of the newly-formed studio near Prague. There he directed his first fully developed puppet film *The Lion and the Tune* in 1959, which won the Grand Prix at the first ASIFA (International Animated Film Association) festival in Annecy, France, in 1960. This puppet pantomine extols poetry, music and art, with its beautifully sculptured three-dimensional characters, and has since become one of the classics of the genre. The production is based on traditional Czech marionettes and established Pojar as the true heir of the Czech puppet tradition.

Many other films followed, but it was *The Apple Tree Maiden* in 1970 which proved to be as outstanding as *The Lion and the Tune*. The handling of the element of supernatural magic in this production, the soft movement, and the visual poetry is typical of Pojar's skill and artistry.

After two anti-war films using the cut-out technique which he made for the United Nations (*Boom* in 1979 and *If* in 1982) he joined forces with the Canadian animator Jacques Drouin in Montreal with the film *The Romance of Darkness*, using Alexeieff and Parker's pin screen technique. He then turned his attention to the *Magic Lantern* and directed an opera based on Jiri Pauer's composition. One of Pojar's interests is making films for children. Bringing his work full circle, he adapted Jiri Trnka's children's book *The Garden* in 1974 and once again has returned to the Trnka tradition which he has so competently retained and expanded during the last thirty years.

Below: *The Little Umbrella* (1957); below left: *If* (1982); opposite page, right: Giersz's *The Horse* (1967); far right: *The Star* (1968)

WITOLD GIERSZ

The qualities that are first noticed in Giersz's films are his mastery of graphic design, his brilliant colour sense and the richly textured painted surfaces. This is due to a reversal of the usual order of animated film production, which tends to begin with a plot which is then developed to put across a gag, a comic situation or to accentuate an animated character. The development in the case of Giersz's films is primarily graphic, its theme dependent solely upon a visual motif emerging from his brushwork. This approach is, in fact, typical of Poland, where graphic design dominates the artistic scene, which has a long tradition derived from posters, stage design and painting. Giersz introduces a fresh approach which delights the eye and heightens our aesthetic sense. Although a former painter, he is surprisingly versatile in film production, being able to adapt himself to the discipline and find new solutions for each film. Each production carries his trademark, his own particular visual ideas.

Giersz was born in Poraj, Poland, in 1927 and he started work in the small town of Bielsko at the local Co-operative Studio. After six years of practice he graduated as a director with the film *The Mystery of the Old Castle* (1956). His major success was achieved with *The Little Western* (1960) which won prizes in many international festivals. The film's originality lies in its strong graphical effects: he did the drawings with a paintbrush and introduced areas of colour in patches with brush strokes, straight onto the celluloid. His technique superseded the conventional 'hard' figures since the manipulation of the patches of colour diffused the outlines of the characters. In *Red and Black* (1963) he concentrated entirely on colour and chromatic visual transformations. *The Horse* (1967) was a wide-screen spectacle; it conveyed a never-ending energetic variation of galloping with constant changes of mobile brush strokes. The feeling of excitement in the dashing animals was immediately transmitted to the audience and the experience proved unforgettable. *The Fire* (1975) evoked the same level of excitement but with the animal power replaced by the force of the elements. Both *The Horse* and *The Fire* have dual themes: both progress through time and space and both have a situation and plot rooted in nature. However, they retain their pure character as animated paintings. *The Fire* is an especially touching film, showing the rebirth of nature after the dynamic destruction of the elements.

JERZY KUCIA

In its early period, animation drew on the comic pages of newspapers and strip cartoons for its graphic style. The animated characters were derived from strip cartoon figures, both animal and human, and the medium was rooted in the most primitive and basic of forms. It was not until the 1920s that the established artists like Léger, Dali, Moholy-Nagy, Duchamp and later Picasso began to experiment in combining static art forms with movement.

Jerzy Kucia is a true successor of that period and is an artist who is totally committed to expressing himself through the motion of his textural shapes without traditional cartoon characters and without 'telling a story'. He is a true expressionist in animated art and aims to reveal the invisible and to witness the passage of time. Emotion plays an important part in his work and his attitude to a problem is to solve it by appealing to the viewers' emotions. If there is also a philosophical message arising out of the experience, so much the better, but it is never an important consideration: what he aims to reveal is his interest in states of mind through the manipulation of abstract forms.

Born in Poland in 1942, Kucia emerged through the Academy of Arts in Warsaw. Choosing to follow a career in film, he gave up the idea of becoming an easel painter of static images. By expressing himself through cinematic language he was aiming for the more immediate contact with the public which he believed only happens via the screen.

Most of Kucia's films are executed in tones of black and white, a style which depends entirely upon effects of light and shade. Starting with a normal, almost monotonous image, he develops it into a panorama of detailed impressions where matters of ordinary life are observed, enlarged and rearranged. This formula is evident in his films *The Barrier* (1977), *Circle* (1978), *Reflections* (1979) and *Chips* (1984), the latter winning him the Grand Prix at the Toronto Animation Festival in 1984. He has only made seven films so far and each one is a step forward from the previous production. With Kucia, the technique is always kept subordinate to the ideas within the film. He considers the technique for each film separately, carefully preparing and researching them according to the subject he is addressing. Each one of his films, he maintains, takes a little bit out of his life.

Above: *Chips* (1984); below: sequences from *Reflections* (1979)

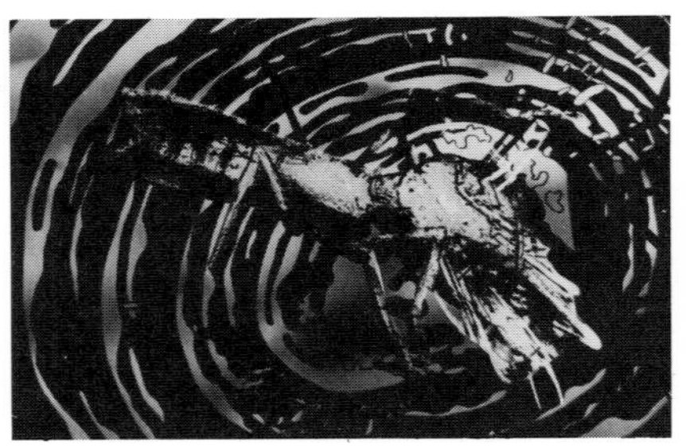

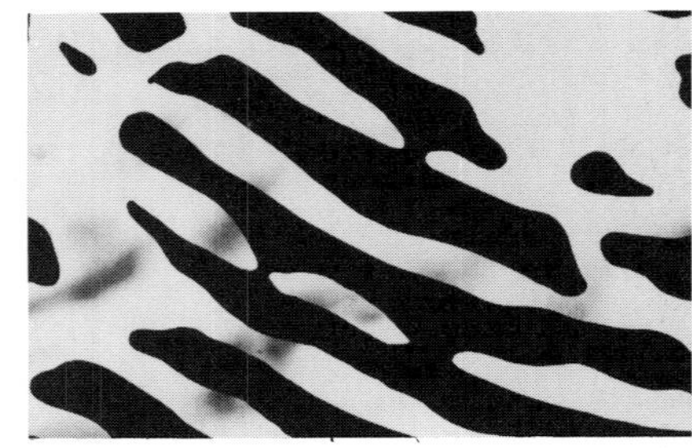

DANIEL SZCZECHURA

Daniel Szczechura, born in Warsaw, Poland, in 1930, entered the world of animation 'through the back door' as it were. Soon after he joined the Academy of Fine Arts he was dismissed for lack of talent. He went on to study History of Art and Film Direction at the State Theatre and Film School in Lodz, where he contributed some ideas and stories for the Students Satirical Theatre. At the same time he tried his hand at making 16mm films, one of which won him a first prize and a position with the Se-Ma-For Studios in Lodz. Nobody could stop Szczechura from then on.

In 1961 he started directing *The Machine* and in 1962 *A Letter*. His next major international success was *The Chair*, in 1963, which won awards in Buenos Aires, Paris, Oberhausen, Cracow and Montevideo, and was a social satire executed with elegant design.

Szczechura is able to build his own surreal worlds into which he invites his audience. This ability is especially evident in *Voyage* (1974) and *Jumping* (1978). The character in *Jumping*, after a very careful routine in the bathroom where he shaves, brushes his hair and makes himself handsome, eats his breakfast, opens the window and jumps out.

Technically and artistically Szczechura is very flexible. He mainly uses collage techniques with paper cut-outs but often utilises cel animation and cut-out photographs. He gives a great deal of attention to pictorial content, which is one of the top priorities in his films. He is a versatile artist with a great variety of stylistic approaches. However, the main consideration is always the basic story with which he likes to shock his audience and involve them both emotionally and intellectually.

It is ironic that at the age of thirty-six he became the very first Professor of Animation at the Academy of Fine Arts where some fifteen years previously he had been dismissed as a student. He is now educating his successors, to the benefit of Polish animation.

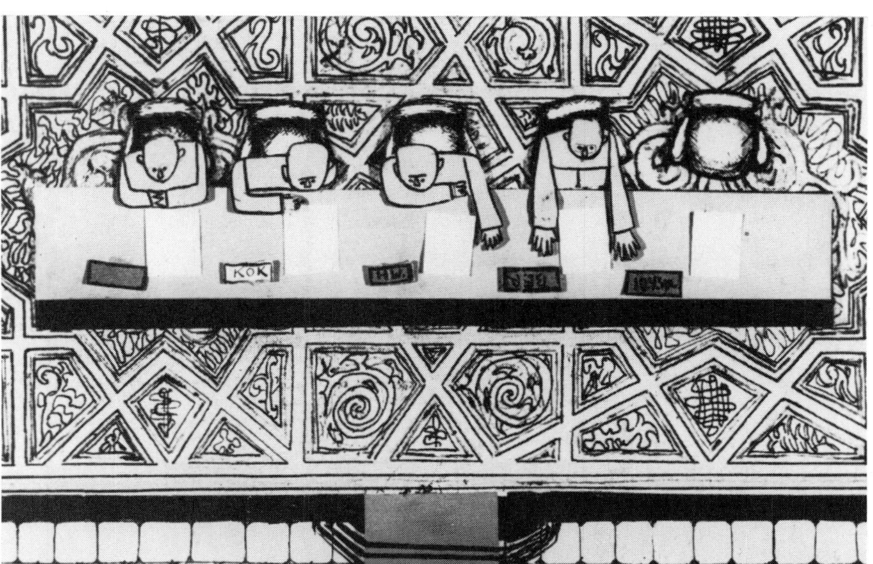

Left: *The Chair* (1963); above left: *Burning Fingers* (1975)

IVAN IVANOV-VANO

One of the founders of Soviet animation was Ivanov-Vano, who was born in Moscow in 1900. Starting work in 1923, his contribution to Soviet animation has since been appreciated all over the world. His first effort as an independent director was in 1927 and he subsequently remained in the forefront of technical and artistic developments in Soviet animation. His style was possibly ahead of its time, but the world (as well as the market) caught up with him to such an extent that he has earned the unofficial title of 'the Russian Disney'. The similarity may lie in the fact that he too recognises that, in order for his films to succeed, they must have 'audience appeal'.

Ivanov-Vano, however, was not satisfied with public acceptance alone. He often adapted his style, experimenting with making films using new techniques and fabrics to obtain additional interest. All of his subjects are based on traditional Russian tales which tap the extremely rich source of local poetry, folk-tales, embroideries, carving and local architecture. Another similarity between him and Disney lies in the scale of the productions which are big, full of spectacular effects, and entirely absorbing. The parallel, however, ends there. Disney stories (which are, as a rule, based on old British and German folk-tales) are diluted to please the widest possible audience. Ivanov-Vano compromises less and retains a purer sense of poetry and aesthetic concepts.

One senses that he really satisfies himself before his audiences.

Out of his wide range of subjects in over fifty years of animated film direction, *The Hunchback Horse* (1947), *The Snow Maiden* (1952), *The Tale of a Dead Princess* (1953) and *Once Upon a Time* (1958) are the most distinguished.

In the sixties he found renewed creative inspiration, which was possibly the result of greater contact with colleagues in the West through festivals organised by the International Animated Film Association (of which he became a vice-president). His film *The Seasons* (1970), based on Tchaikovsky's music, was an imaginative and colourful interpretation of the contrasting Russian landscape, but the most powerful and best designed of his films was *The Battle of Kerchenetz*, based on a traditional opera with the music of Rimsky-Korsakov. The film is an outstanding example of the fusion of old Russian icons, with their brilliant transparent colour and elegant design, and the rhythms of music, also making excellent use of time and space and dynamic film cutting. The treatment of the sequence where the battle subsides and the peasants return to their land has a lyricism which is quite outstanding in colour and poetic mood. Yuri Norstein, a young film-maker and disciple of Ivanov-Vano, co-directed this film and has since made his way independently.

Through his unique approach to animation, Ivanov-Vano has contributed to Russian art as significantly as any of the great Russian composers, dramatists or novelists.

Right: *The Magic Lake* (1979); above right: *The Hunchback Horse* (1947); opposite page, top: *The Battle of Kerchenetz* (1971); bottom: *The Tale of a Dead Princess* (1953)

YURI NORSTEIN

Born in Andreyevskiy, Russia, in 1941, Yuri Norstein worked for years under the tutelage of the veteran Russian animator Ivanov-Vano, and has emerged as one of the world's leading animators. His last film *The Tale of Tales* was considered by many to be the most artistic production so far to emerge from Eastern Europe in the eighties. The success of this film, as well as others of his like *The Vixen and the Hare* (1973), *The Heron and the Crane* (1974) and *The Hedgehog in the Fog* (1975), is due to his unique style. He creates multi-dimensional figures and backgrounds which have depth, roundness and shading, giving a visual quality to his pictures seldom seen in other films. His stories are full of minute observations, contrasting a wide range of emotions from gaiety and laughter through to sadness and disappointment. The fact that these moods are felt by animals and birds within their own particular environment provides an enchanting element of believable magic and once again proves that the art of animation can bridge the barrier between the human and animal worlds.

Norstein considers animation to be a new field of art but one which is still seriously underestimated. He claims

that its artistic flexibility and social significance have not yet been fully explored.

Apart from being an animator, Norstein is also a good painter and a brilliant illustrator, which explains the high quality of his backgrounds and the expressions of his characters. He has a close relationship with his young children and considers their reactions carefully before making a film. He thinks that only those who understand the psychology of children should make films for them: if one has sympathy and can play with them, one is able to look at the world through their minds and eyes.

He also thinks that, ideally, animated film directors should be interested in the fine arts, especially painting, since films have a dual objective: the creation of a new and original setting and the development of action within that setting. He recognises that a film is usually composed of a variety of elements: it can contain myth, fantasy, ideas, sound, realism and naturalism. The specific mixture of these elements could be of great value, lifting animation above all other media, but so far he has not seen any film, short or long, which has made full use of such potential. He thinks that feature-length films should not only tell stories but present the richness of human life, making full use of the specific properties of animation.

Looking at Norstein's animation one feels that he has successfully put his ideas across on screen already. He still has plenty of ideas to explore within the Russian literary tradition, however, and enters the fantasy world of Gogol in the classic story *The Coat*, scheduled for release in 1988.

Right: *The Heron and the Crane* (1974); above right: *The Tale of Tales* (1982); opposite page, top: *The Hedgehog in the Fog* (1975); left: *The Coat*

FEODOR KHITRUK

Khitruk is one of the best-known animators and teachers of animation in Russia. His output may not be as prolific as Ivanov-Vano's and his style not quite as robust, but his wit and humour are just as outstanding, although more internal and personal. He chooses his subjects out of ordinary, everyday life, pin-points human weaknesses with shrewd observation and allows his audiences to draw their own conclusions.

He was born in Kalinize, Russia, in 1917 and joined the studio of Soyuzmultfilm as an animator in 1937. After working on a great number of films directed by others, he at last began to direct his own in 1959. *The Story of the Crime* (1963) revealed his sharply critical views about human weaknesses as did a satire on the film industry called *Film, Film, Film*, made in 1968.

His interest in animation for children is demonstrated in films such as *Bonifacio's Holiday* (1965) and an adaptation of A. A. Milne's *Winnie the Pooh* (1969). Both productions differ from the mass-produced Hollywood and Japanese television cartoons through the detailed attention to characterisation and the introduction of good graphics in figure design.

One of his outstanding films, based on Shakespeare's five-act tragedy *Othello* (1967), lasts all of fifty-five seconds. The film is designed as a modern pastiche of Elizabethan etching and is a high-speed parody of American-styled television commercials. Its visual shorthand becomes a sharp comment on our times and it won the major film prize in Montreal in 1967.

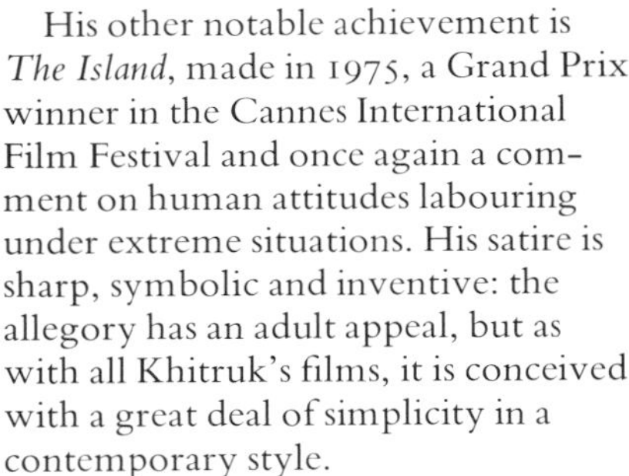

His other notable achievement is *The Island*, made in 1975, a Grand Prix winner in the Cannes International Film Festival and once again a comment on human attitudes labouring under extreme situations. His satire is sharp, symbolic and inventive: the allegory has an adult appeal, but as with all Khitruk's films, it is conceived with a great deal of simplicity in a contemporary style.

One of his latest films is *The Lion and the Bull* (1984). He side-steps his usual approach as a satirist and tries his hand at a drama based on the theme of power. The two animals confront each other for ultimate supremacy. The outcome is exciting and the design distinguished, but many of his fans still wish he would return to his superb satire from which it is possible to learn so much about human attitudes.

At present, Khitruk teaches at the Moscow Academy and is the President of the Animation Association of twenty-five studios in the fifteen different nations around the Soviet Union.

Above left: *Film, Film, Film* (1968); below: *Toptychka* (1964); below left: *A Young Man Called Engels* (1976)

REIN RAAMAT

Estonia is one of the smallest of the Soviet republics, having its own tradition reflecting more its Gothic past than classic Russian culture. Its people have developed a high degree of craftsmanship in carving, sculpture, puppetry and the theatre. Rein Raamat came from this stable as a young graduate of the Tallinn Institute of Art.

He joined the new studio in Tallinn soon after the war. His first task was to design sets and characters for stop-motion puppet films. In a small studio one often has to fulfil the functions of script-writer, puppet-maker and set-decorator, and in the process he gained the experience to become a director.

By the sixties, together with two other directors of puppet films at Tallinn, Elbert Tuganov and Heino Pars, he had produced a number of entertaining puppet films which were especially notable for their simple and economic execution. By that time the studio had expanded its activities towards the more complex forms of animated cartoon techniques and was starting to be noticed in festivals around the world.

Bridging the difference between three-dimensional puppetry and two-dimensional animation on celluloid is not quite as simple as it may appear. The former has the advantage of easy recognition on account of the plasticity of puppets which are much easier for the eye to identify (particularly in a region where the tradition goes back for centuries). In graphic animation, the lack of this has to be compensated for by other qualities. Story-telling becomes more difficult because the director has to communicate with symbols and painted forms which require a more careful continuity, whereas some effects (such as metamorphosis) become easier in flat animation, although the action requires a speedier development. Raamat has studied the myriad differences between the two mediums and understands exactly how to manipulate them both to advantage.

In his first internationally acknowledged film *Flight* (1973) the subject is the desire to reach higher and higher, and Raamat makes good use of the fact that one is able to defy gravity in animated movies. In his subsequent production *The Archer*, made in 1974 (a film about a whale hunter who, when his line breaks and he is almost drowned, is saved by the whale he was trying to kill), he completely reversed his style from light, flowing figures to heavily textured, powerful ones. This was also evident in his next film *Antenna on Ice* (1977) which conveys force and muscle power as a man struggles against the elements.

In *Tyll the Giant* (1980) the conflict is between human beings and supernatural monsters: the conflict is superbly dramatic, as is the design of the monsters. His latest film *Hell* (1983) also contains some elements of the supernatural in both story and character design. Based on the etchings of Edward Viiralt, an Estonian artist, the film tells the story of a character's condemnation to Hell as a punishment for consenting to carnal sin. It is almost an animated version of Hieronymus Bosch's *Garden of Earthly Delights*, having many surreal episodes. It is inspiring to see that such rich, individual styles are in existence throughout the USSR.

Above: *Hell* (1983); left: *The Archer* (1974)

PAUL DRIESSEN

Paul Driessen is a highly original artist whose work is instantly recognisable. His films have three basic elements which differentiate them from the work of other animators: the free, loose drawings resembling scribbles, which could just as well come from the pen of a gifted child; the fact that his stories are not for children but primarily have adult appeal; and the emphasis on humour which is purely visual. He makes a character out of a dot and plays with contrasting dimensions and absurd or whimsical fantasies. Added to this, his graphic treatment of contrasting black and white tonal forms provides a visual vibration on the screen seldom achieved before.

Paul Driessen was born in Nijmegen, Holland, in 1940. After a turbulent early life during the years when Holland was the battleground of Europe, he became a graphic designer having studied at the Academy of Arts in Utrecht, and started work in a small studio in Hilversum on animated films for television. There, in 1964, he met the American animator Jim Hiltz, who gave him his first chance to learn the technicalities of the art.

Driessen feels he is lucky not to have known anything about animation up to that time, since it meant that he was not influenced by any style. Thereafter he truly earned the label 'The Flying Dutchman': in 1967 he worked on *The Yellow Submarine* in London, and in 1968 he made his first film *The Story of Little John Bailey* in Holland. In 1970 he went to Canada and since then has commuted between the National Film Board of Canada and his studio in Holland, where he works with the producer Nico Crama. He has made two outstanding films with Crama, *The Killing of an Egg* (1976) and *David* (1977), adding to the steady, excellent output of his personal films.

He recognises and appreciates the differences between the two continents. In Holland he enjoys the quiet isolation of working alone; in Canada he likes the contact with other animators and the excellent equipment available. The unifying themes in his films are the idiosyncratic visual imagery, the abstract cartoon ideas and the mystical content of the stories. He categorises his films into: Crazy Tendencies (productions like *Cat's Cradle* and *On Land, At Sea and In the Air*); Short Gags (works like *The Killing of an Egg*, *Elbowing* and *Oh What a Knight*); Dramatic Structures (films such as *An Old Box*, *David* and *Spotting a Cow*). Visual comedy plays a significant role in all of them. He states:

'I like spending time on my back in the sun, dreaming up new ideas; a small but important part of my schedule. So little time, so much to do . . .'

Top: *David* (1977); above: *Oh What a Knight* (1982); below: *Cat's Cradle* (1974)

PART THREE

THE MODERN AGE

COMPUTERS AND THE NEW LOOK

If 'comic strip animation' was the new art form for the beginning of the twentieth century, computer animation must surely be the popular medium for the century's closing years. Originally, the tool of the animator was paper, pencil and ink. Today's materials are the electronic stylus and the flickering screen of the television tube. For the new generation, self-identity is expressed more naturally through this medium than any other. Both methods, new and old, are dependent on the progression of time and space, but here one may just as well pause, since the scale and variety of expression has widened to such an extent that there is little else to unite them.

There are two aspects to consider here, the range of expression and the stylistic options of the new tools. At the beginning, when everything that moved appeared to be magic, comedy (usually of the slapstick variety) was the ultimate aim of most cartoonists and cartoonist/performers. If there was an element of fantasy or a complex idea in their work, it was a bonus. An animated cartoon could satisfy audiences with the most basic techniques simply by making them laugh. As time and techniques progressed, the dimension of expression grew; the invention of the soundtrack, for instance, added not only words but music. Innovative techniques opened the way for the new 'graphic art' look in animated cartoons. Visual representations of the subconscious, sensuality and surrealism became fashionable. Abstractions and the absurd were added; allegory, drama, poetry, parody and satire became possible, as did the metamorphosis of one form into another; these features began to provide the visual stimuli which today are an integral diet for our eyes, our brains and our nervous systems, which are now conditioned to the quick perception of images and instant recognition of symbols.

While the formats of other arts have remained comparatively stable, the art of animated film has undergone considerable growth and transition in the second half of the twentieth century. This is an expansion which even other forms of entertainment (including normal live-action cinematography and stage techniques) have not experienced. However, it is not at the limit, and may only be at the beginning, of its potential. As new tools arrive in the field of animated picture-making, the field is constantly widening. More than the range of human expression, the range of tools which are available to modern animators is bewildering. Painters since the Renaissance have used brush, paint and canvas. An animator, whether working in two or three dimensions, has the option of using many different materials and several hundred visual effects to create the final look of the work. The material may consist of literally any substance which can be manipulated in frame-by-frame film animation.

The photographic camera techniques which have evolved throughout the 1970s and 1980s contain a long list of special effects with optical camera equipment. Even before the computer-generated design techniques, the palette for visual imagery had become a very complex science of its own.

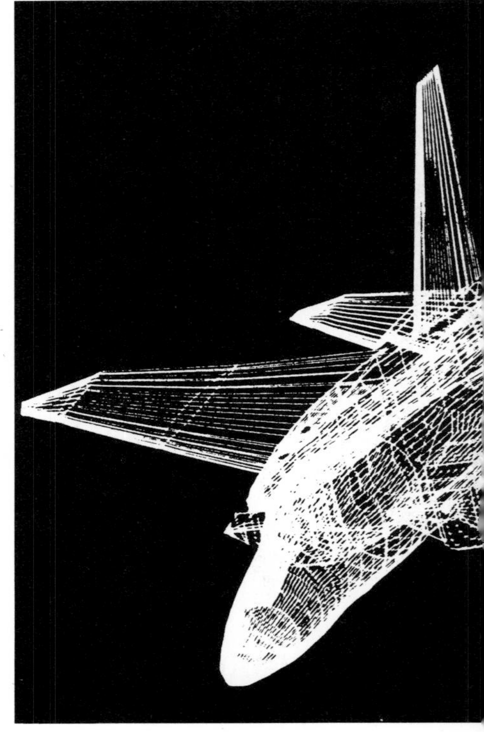

The same applies to the techniques for the production of soundtracks, in recording electronically-produced musical effects and human voices. Such expansion of available material and variety of techniques in photography and recording could be, of course, a mixed blessing. It does require a discipline in the animator: an essential understanding of what could be achieved by the various materials and techniques at one's disposal. But as soon as one has acquired an overall comprehension of what these are all about, it can provide unlimited possibilities for creating something new and exciting which has never before been seen or experienced in any other art media.

Computer animation, the latest newcomer of drawing techniques, has attracted a great deal of attention. To understand how a drawn image can express so much life and movement is puzzling enough, but how a machine can be used to create pictures of such complex nature as those seen on television is even more perplexing. Indeed the process is extremely specialised and even now, after some twenty years of development, only relatively few people understand it and practise the method.

Possibly the first practical use of computer animation was in a meteorological department in the USA, which drew maps over the Arctic Circle showing the rapid movement of air mass as it expanded. The motion was updated every hour, and used in weather forecasting, and a variation of such use has been introduced in the Meteorological Office of Great Britain, as well as by the weather forecasting section of both ITV and BBC TV.

Below: part of a computer-generated simulation of an aircraft in flight (used for training pilots) by Evans and Sutherland

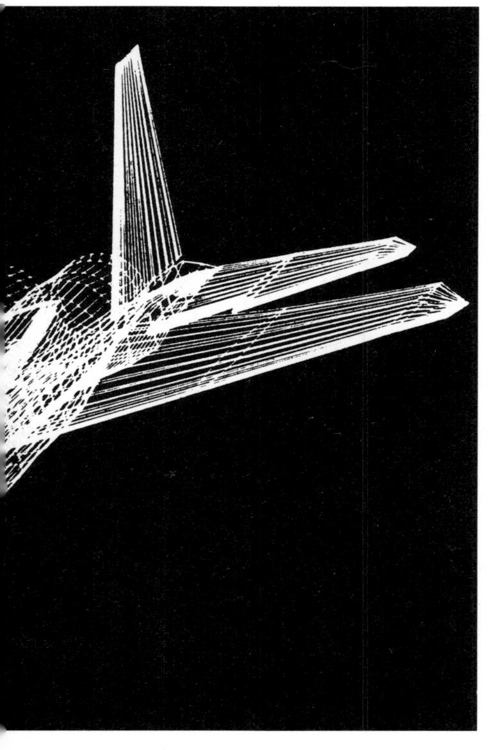

This early application in the USA developed into a national defence system. Several hundred television sets were installed in military bases on which personnel could watch any objects flying within 700 miles of the coast. Enemy aircraft could not only be traced, their speed and altitude could also be detected and followed on the Cathode Ray Tube (CRT). This was one of the first instances of animated graphics on the computer. It is perhaps disturbing to realise that the first significant advances were developed for military, and not creative, purposes.

Computer graphics, both static and animated, proved to be highly useful. A pioneer computer engineer called Dr Evans (who later with another computer scientist, Dr Sutherland, established the most distinguished hardware company for computers) has introduced a comparatively simple method to draw images with a computer. It consists of 'electronic tablets' on which one can draw using 'light pens', keyboards and video recorders attached to the computer. The whole thing is a neat and tidy unit which is quite manageable when the technique has been learnt. The idea took off, both in the USA and in Britain, and the use of it soon developed in two directions. One of them is the highly useful application of it in fields such as human engineering; design analysis; scientific studies; medical simulation; mathematical investigations and experiments with aerodynamic and physical concepts. In the latter example, for instance, there are studies going on into 'destructive testing': instead of blowing up a 747 aeroplane to investigate the weak points, it can be done graphically on a computer, with the relevant conditions and stresses methodically applied. One can then watch the whole process and make modifications in the design accordingly.

An interesting aspect of the scientific application is in the study of objects which are too small or too big for the naked eye to see. Scientists think and calculate in microseconds and light years, a hugely contrasting range of concepts: now, time itself can be effectively shown and handled, enlarged and expanded with the aid of computers. It can also be compressed in a similar manner. In a remarkable experimental video production called 'Galaxy' made in the late sixties, the University of Syracuse in New York State compressed 200 billion years of galaxy formation into three minutes of action. The plotting of the path of thousands and thousands of stars as they converged into new planets was not only a scientific statement but also a very exciting visual experience.

Inevitably, all of these specific, practical applications were developed before any artistic ones. In the early days of the computer, the major advances took place in universities, which were able to provide so many essential aspects for research: money, knowledge, time and patience, plus, of course, a vested interest in finding new ways of teaching and learning. The first results emerged from the universities of Utah, Salt Lake City; Cornell University in New York; Syracuse; Toronto and, in Britain, Edinburgh and Manchester. Soon, institutes followed such as one in Massachusetts; the New York Institute of Technology and the Brooklyn Polytechnic Institute. A number of special laboratories were set up for experimental research, like the Atlas at Harwell, the IBM Scientific Center in Los Angeles and the General Electric Company's Electronic Laboratory in New York. Privately owned organisations spending their own money, such as the Computer Image Corporation in Denver and Antics in London, were at a disadvantage when it came to the millions of dollars invested by big corporations such as IBM and the universities, whose resources for research were practically endless. As a consequence of this gigantic development of computer technology, nothing could stop progress. Meanwhile, there were some significant contributions by individual inventors which cannot be ignored and which will be dealt with later.

The second stream of development embraces the less utilitarian side of computer animation. It consists of experiments in a variety of areas: in animated cartoons; advertising graphics; entertainment and abstract visual forms in search of a new artistic medium. There were some fine works done by artists during the pre-computer period with electronic oscilloscopes and many found it quite easy to understand the computer and continue their activities with the newer equipment.

As the engineering aspect of computer graphics entered into more and more complex areas and evolved into different systems, it moved further and further away from the tradition of 'art-work'. One of the problems to be solved was how to make it easier for the artist to manipulate the

Right: 'System IV' a 'real time' instant animation system developed by Harrison Lee III of Computer Images Corporation, USA

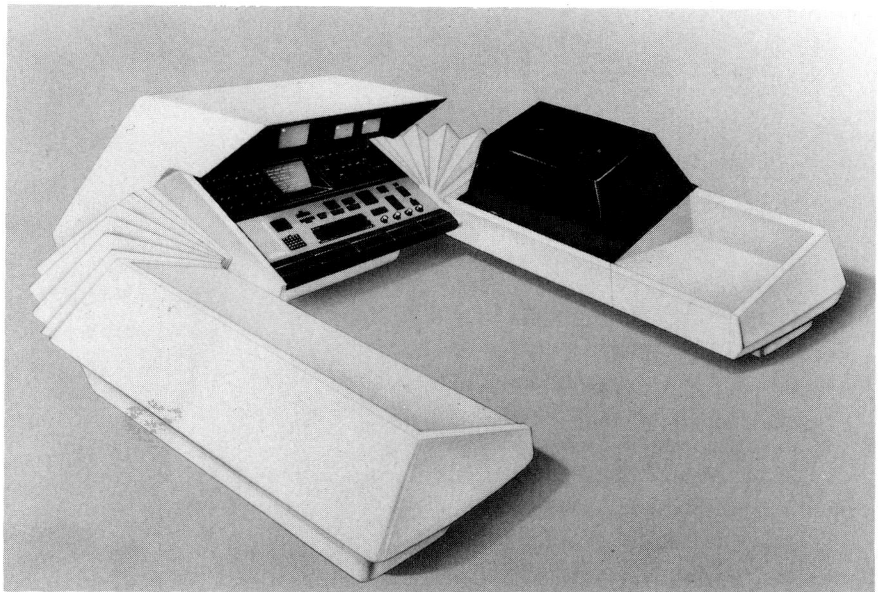

machine. In time, the facilities were developed to obtain millions of shades of colours and millions of tones from black to white. It became possible to distort the shape of an object endlessly, enlarge it or make it smaller and perform seemingly magical deeds without anyone having to learn complex mathematics and computer terminology. What was not solved, however, was the psychological attitude of many artists, who developed an anti-machine phobia in handling an electronic stylus in the place of a graphite pencil. Yet a computer should not be an awesome thing. It is really only a tightly-packed, electronic combination of wires, with a silicon chip for a nerve centre and all it deals in are 'bits' which are switched on or off. At the same time, of course, it is also one of the most powerful tools on earth, if one can address it in a language it is able to understand. One might have assumed that there would be a unified language created, specifically geared to communicating with computers. After all, there are some universal forms of communication: music, ballet, the visual arts and mathematics all make use of them. Computer languages used in software, however, are not amongst them. Unfortunately, there are virtually hundreds of computer languages, all different from each other, which is confusing, unhelpful and wasteful. In just over twenty years, the computer industry has produced a modern babel. Many software packages are similar, but most of them are unusable on other machines: every major company has gone its own way, and as time has developed, become increasingly isolated. From the point of view of major companies and research organisations, the argument is based on purely commercial considerations. Many of them have spent vast sums of money and it is simply not in their interests to promote communication.

It also appears that the more complex the computer becomes, the greater need there is for artist-computer interaction. Interaction, as the description implies, refers to the human intervention in a program, whether graphically (by means of a keyboard) or pictorially (using a light pen and 'drawing' directly onto an electronic tablet). This means that the artist's work can be seen at the same time as he or she creates it, corrections can be made instantly and the work stored for future repeats, if necessary. By the early seventies, practically all computer graphics work followed more or less the same sequential process of action but, as referred to previously, using a slightly different software formula evolved and developed by each establishment. These differences were jealously guarded by the computer programmers and marketed commercially like any other valuable product.

The name of Dr Charles Csuri is widely-known in the world of computer animation. As the Head of the Arts Department of Ohio State University, he produced *Sketchbook*, a twenty-five-minute film with colour and sound. The features to be tackled in the process were: a solution to 'hidden line' problems (i.e. making a moving line disappear when passing 'behind' another line); 'real-time' (instantly visible) manipulation; multiple independent movements and the addition of colour and solid areas. There was also the question of how to combine live-action photography with computerised images. The equipment consisted of two standard IBM machines: the 1130 system adapted for animation and the 2250 display unit. These machines were big and very expensive – since then smaller, more efficient ones have been designed especially for animation work.

The method employed in such a project is as follows: the artist draws the very first and the very last key images onto the IBM 2250 Cathode Ray Tube with a light pen. These are stored and the computer programs (which have been previously prepared) are called up. They perform the following actions: they produce all the drawings in between the first and the last positions; they handle the 'hidden line' problem (described above); they cause the image to follow a predetermined path (which could be established mathematically or drawn on the CRT); and they cause independent motion of any segment of the image defined as a separate entity. Finally, as the image is moving on the CRT the artist may change or modify the motion of all or any part of the image by using the function keys. For tonal variation, the grey scale for solid colour is produced by varying the point density on the 2250 display unit.

The images have to be filmed in stop-motion, due to insufficient speed in the painting: the black and white pictures are fed into a video recorder and the final colour film is produced by the use of filters. Today, the colour palette is built into the computer as an integral part of the machine.

About the same time as Dr Csuri's production of *Sketchbook*, Dr Becker at the University of Maryland made *Genesis I*. This production was made with a Massachusetts Institute of Technology TX-2 Computer with Dr Becker's own Genesis software program, a CRT, an electronic tablet

Above: two frames from the title sequence of *ABC News* by Cranston Csuri Productions, USA: early three-dimensional simulated shapes designed and processed by Dr Charles Csuri

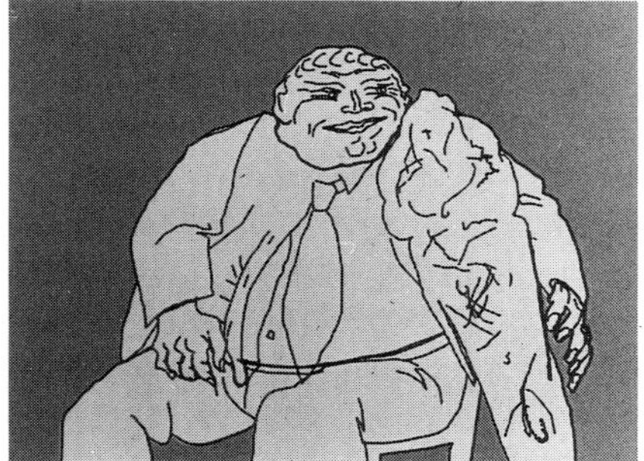

Above: four frames from *Hunger* by Peter Foldes

and, of course, a light pen. The method employed was virtually a standard operation. The artist drew the images on to the electronic tablet and saw the image simultaneously appearing on the CRT. By pressing keys or pointing the command boxes on the CRT, each image was stored in the computer and recalled at will. To indicate pathways, the artist described the path on the tablet: this image appeared on the CRT in the form of a dotted line. The faster the action of the drawing, the closer were the dots, and the playback motion effectively duplicated the artist's actions. To move or change the start or the end points, the artist defined the picture with the pen on the tablet, following the changes on the CRT, altering or replacing the individual frames if necessary. The entire sequence could be played back at high speed before filming.

The late sixties and the early seventies were a most exciting period for the development of computer animation, both from the point of view of technical advancement and artistic achievements. The two cultures began working constructively with each other. For instance, Dr Ken Knowlton, an expert in computer technology from the Bell Telephone Laboratories, teamed up with Lillian Schwartz, a talented abstract painter, and jointly produced *Pixilation*, a three-minute experiment in geometrical manipulation, with computerised music by Gershon Kingsley. This interesting partnership lasted for a decade and Lillian Schwartz is still 'painting with computers'. There was also the partnership of Dr Citron of IBM Scientific Center with one of the great experimentalists of American cinema, John Whitney Snr, who with Dr Citron's CAMP programme did the films *Permutations* and *Matrix I* at the Californian Institute of Technology. Both films broke new ground: the latter proving a strong relationship between mathematics, graphic movement and music.

Another impressive partnership involved Peter Foldés, a Hungarian painter who worked with the National Film Board of Canada in 1977. He made his film *Hunger* in the University of Toronto with two computer scientists, Dr Burtnyk and Dr Wein. Apart from the dramatic impact of the film and its excellent visual quality, it was a breakthrough in modelling techniques: characters were able to fall and rise freely in the air and rotate around themselves creating a three-dimensional illusion. In 1981, I myself made the film *Dilemma* in conjunction with the Computer Creation Corporation in the USA. This took the illusion a step further by introducing a sophisticated shading system laid over the colour of the forms and objects, resulting in a rich visual experience. The story contrasted the creation and development of civilisation up to the present day with our relatively recent potential for complete destruction within seconds. Such close co-operation between computer experts, film-makers and designers is the basis of all progress in computer animation.

Today, the question of interaction between the artist and the tools is less of a stumbling block. Dick Shoup, of Aurora Images in San Francisco, is another pioneer in bringing the two levels of the function closer, for which

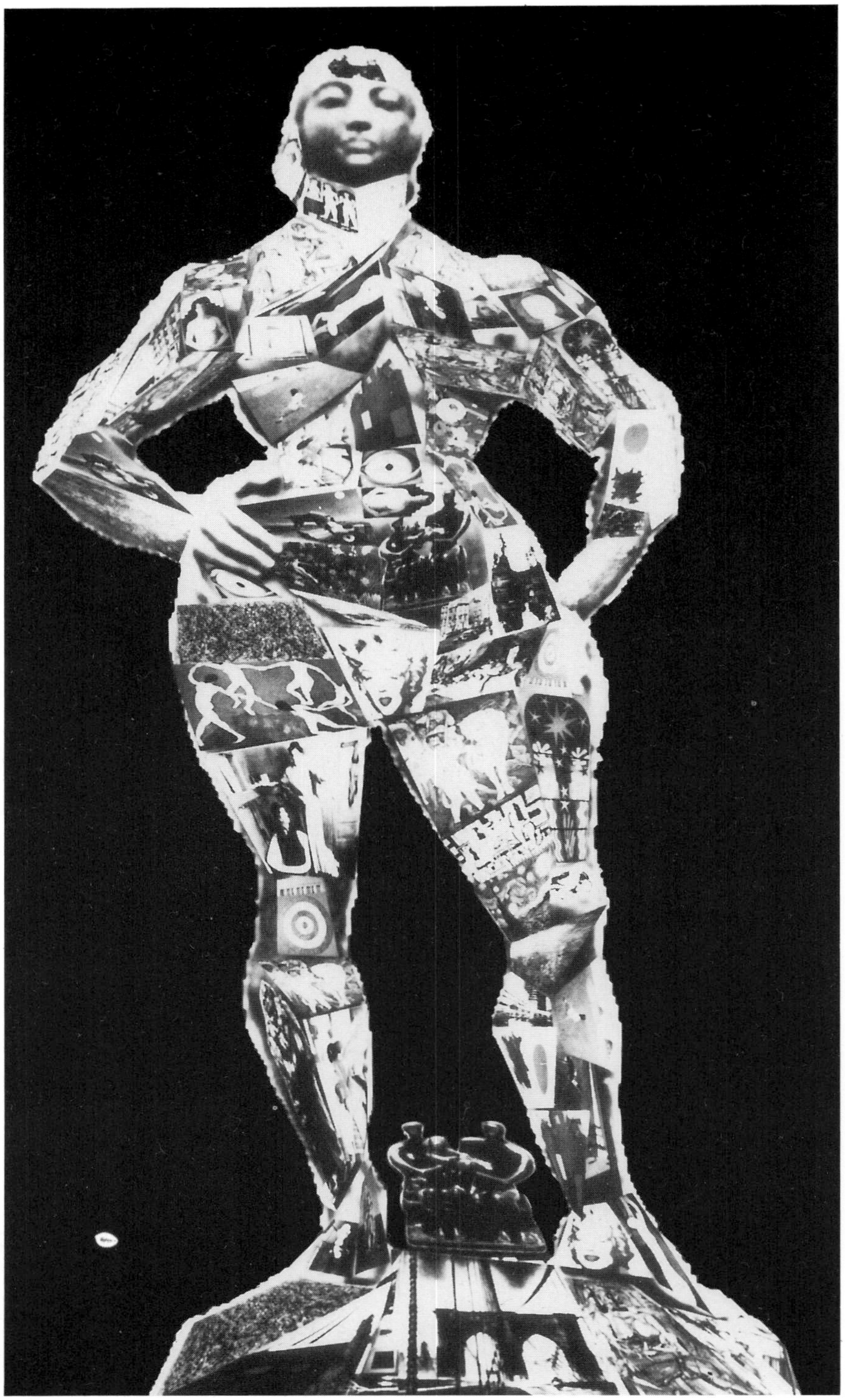

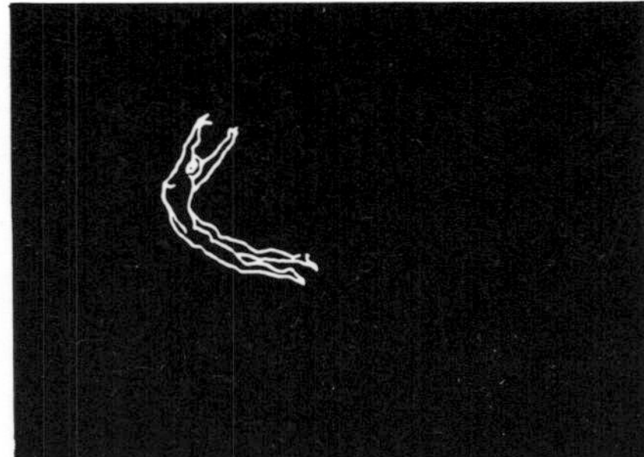

Left: *Lily in Computer Land*, a picture of the artist's life and work in electronic animation, by Lillian Schwartz; above: three frames from *Metadata* by Peter Foldes

he received the Academy of Arts Emmy Award in 1984. He simply constructed a visually based 'menu' which functions through a command button. The name of 'menu' is a simplified computer term especially designed to help animators choose a predetermined action by touching a button. The action can be seen as it takes shape in front of their eyes in very much the same way as putting down a shape with a pencil on paper. In this case, the way one activates the command on the menu is by pin-pointing it with a stylus pen on the electronic tablet. Consequently the stylus becomes the most important drawing instrument in the process.

Above: two of the images from *Dilemma* (1981), directed by the author and designed by Janos Kass, in conjunction with the Computer Creation Corporation, USA

What is actually on the menu is, of course, vitally important when the artist selects the ingredients. The menu could offer, for instance, eighty functions, but several hundred more if someone specially prepares them. Whilst this method may sound simple, it is not quite so straightforward when it goes into operation. The computer is a highly complex machine responding to electronic signals. The monitor, which is the instant play-back screen, displays a 'cursor' which shows where the stylus is pointing on the tablet and acts as a guide between the coordinated functions of the artist's hand and eye. Essentially, Dick Shoup's innocent-looking menu hides the whole technological evolution which has taken place in the last quarter of a century with Dr Zajac and Dr Knowlton's early experiments.

However brilliant a computer graphic system may be, without someone creative to visualise it, it cannot be put into full effect. A whole cycle of events is required to create the results which are expected by audiences today: the machines which depend on engineers; the systems which depend on the programmers and the performance which depends on the animator. Here we have a three-layer sandwich structure, which could not hold together without the distinct layers of ingredients it requires (although it is quite feasible for the engineer to become a programmer or for the animator to also do the programming function). This sandwich analogy indicates that there are not two cultures to expand the technology but three. The first is 'machine intelligence': the language capacity built into the computer enabling it to carry out a complex series of operations; an area in which the United States has been enjoying a tradition of excellence and where so much has been contributed through the work of research institutes and universities. The second consists of the software experts (programmers and engineers) who make the machine function and the third is made up of the people who are actually creating the pictures on the screen – possibly the most neglected layer of the sandwich.

TELEVISION GRAPHICS

It is interesting to note that in spite of the gigantic input into computer technology by major corporations, research institutes, universities and hardware manufacturers, it was not until the late seventies that the two major users of this genre – the television and advertising industries – started to take up computer animation in a big way.

Within a comparatively short space of time, audiences around the world were suddenly introduced to shapes and forms previously unfamiliar to them through television announcements, titles and commercials. They saw titles which zoomed towards the foreground from out of nowhere, letters which turned upside down, objects which radiated, sparkled and twisted, products which turned, leapt, soared into the air and then disintegrated, only to reassemble seconds later, radiating and shining. All these effects occurred at lightning speed with a colour palette of incredible richness. Few people realised that these dazzling, texturised images were examples of the new animation. In the cinema, satellites whizzing past both sides of the enlarged screen zoomed into the far distance at incredible speeds, somersaulted and flew right into the camera. Dazzling lighting effects pulsated on to the screen with ear-splitting sound effects. It is a long way from Bugs Bunny but no matter. It is a contemporary branch of animation which enabled the science fiction film industry to expand, the television industry to get more interesting and the advertising industry to become yet more prosperous.

With its high turnover of programmes, television needs a streamlined system to introduce, advertise and present programmes with the maximum visual impact in the shortest possible time. But there are certain rules to this game. Since the very start of television, animators have realised that television graphics is an art of its own with little reference to two-dimensional graphics. The reason for such a difference lies in the nature of the television medium itself. The electronic process involves transition, recording and reception, each of which can influence the final look of a design. The climax is the final appearance of the work on a sensitive fluorescent tube interlined with a complex line reference. The image only appears momentarily in the form of light, which is, therefore, one of the working materials.

The range of assignments for television graphics widened considerably during the seventies and eighties. Apart from an increasing number of animated children's films, titles, television advertising spots, and science programmes, the biggest increase occurred in brief announcements giving advance publicity to forthcoming programmes. The majority are conceived in the form of moving graphics in conjunction with live images backed by verbal messages. The objective is to make an instant impact with memorable, impressive graphics. Titles and captions, however, are still the main requirements for television programmes, as are the substantial graphics for news and variety, weather report, sports and music programmes. It is worth noting that the tendency is to use less and less words in the introduction of these programmes and an ever increasing amount of visual images. The

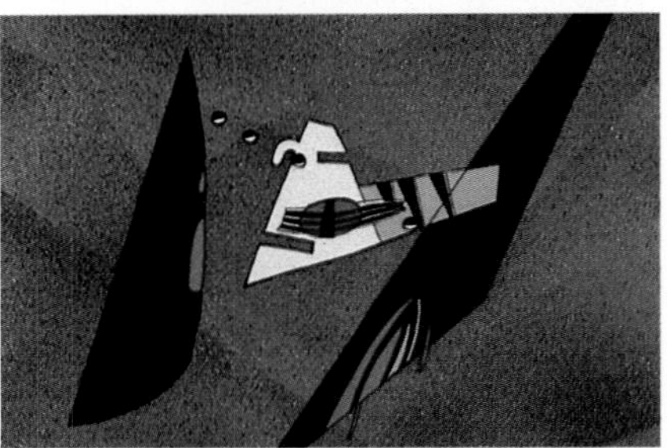

Above: promotional graphics for *Jazz on a Summer's Day* by the BBC Presentation department, designed by Graham Kern

Opposite page, right: opening title sequence for BBC TV's *Sports Night*, designed by Darrell Pockett; centre: opening title sequence for BBC TV's *Young Musician of the Year*, designed by Liz Friedman; far right: CBC's *La Flèche du Temps*, designed by André Théroux

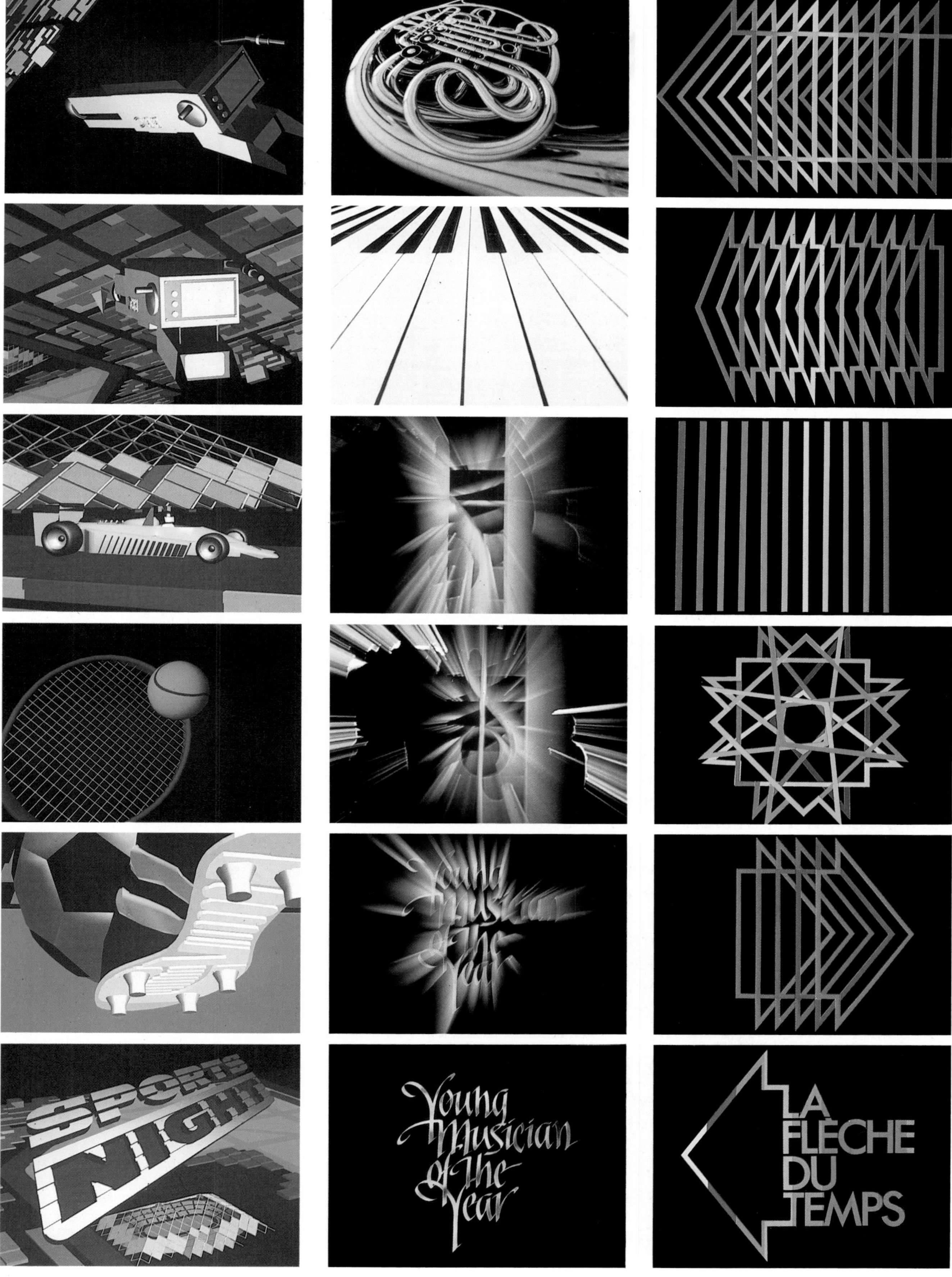
SPORTS
NIGHT
Young
Musician
of The
Year
LA
FLÈCHE
DU
TEMPS

integration of drawn and live images with the further elements of movement and sound can convey a message very powerfully indeed.

A further interesting factor is that the new generation of television graphic designers have discovered the potential of visual metamorphosis which permits them to transform one visual shape into another one by means of motion. These transitions (such as the conversion of abstract configurations of lines into actual letters) acquire a specific meaning of their own, and could even lead to the development of a new kinetic art form. In the rapidly developing electronic communication system, this field is one where the new generation of animators will find the greatest expansion as well as the most difficult challenge.

To outline a few examples, John Aston, Graphic Design Manager for BBC TV, works with a number of first-class designers such as Haydon Young, Darrell Pockett, Liz Jones and Liz Friedman. These and other artists have created memorable introductory titles and sequences for programmes like the 1984 Olympiad and *Sports Night*, conceived with a combination of complex techniques and ingenious skill.

Hubert Tison, Head Designer at CBC in Montreal, Canada, has a world-wide reputation for his team which includes Frédéric Back, Graeme Ross and André Théroux. Their work always attains a high level of graphic invention, using the latest available tools to carry them out, generating exciting effects and a feeling of visual freshness. Hans-Jürgen Donner, an Austrian-born graphic artist, has produced a number of well-conceived and very contemporary titles for TV Globo in Rio de Janeiro, using the computer facilities of the New York Institute of Technology to carry through his ideas. Another significant name in this field is Pat Gavin, of London Weekend Television, who has contributed a great deal to the overall quality of programmes themselves. He too has made full use of the electronic medium by the introduction of a sense of 'electrified' excitement in his sequence titles. His early use of skilful typography was apparent in the opening titles for the comedy series *Freddie Starr's Variety Madhouse*, animated by himself and John Miller. He also combines traditional cartoon techniques with computer animation, as in the highly acclaimed opening titles for *The South Bank Show* and the inventive science fiction element in *20th Century Box*. Gavin has shown how one can successfully combine the old optical camera techniques with the richness and diversity of the new electronic systems.

Good television graphics, however, are not confined to Britain, Canada and the USA. France, Germany, Finland and (especially) Dutch television stations like NOS and VARA are also aware of the magnetic effect of computer-generated titles.

As new equipment reaches the market, the television graphics industry is in an admirable position to further enrich its capabilities with a more colourful palette and varieties of textures and shapes which would not be possible with the traditional tools of animation.

ANIMATED ADVERTISING

Once the advertising industry discovered the value of computer animation it became one of the major users of the medium on television, integrating graphics with live action. Within a short space of time, advertising had become a considerable stimulus to computer animation for two main reasons. It has 'impossible' demands (such as wanting to endow a product with human characteristics) which only animation can solve, and it has the money to pay experts to carry out further visual experiments in developing new ideas. Consequently some of the most spectacular computer animation has been produced in the form of advertising spots on television.

This form of art has even created its own brand of heroes. Among them are Robert Abel in Hollywood; Richard and Robert Greenberg and Judson Rosebush in New York; Alvy Ray Smith, James Blinn and Lance Williams (all of whom contributed much to the development of the genre as a visual tool); and Cranston and Csuri, who successfully utilised their scientific and academic background for commercial purposes. To open a computerised animation studio, it is not enough simply to be a graphic genius. One must know and understand the latest advances made in computer technology and be capable of refreshing one's own software to keep up with the competition. One must also have the necessary financial resources to install new equipment and adapt these for newer effects to improve the technical quality of the work. As a rule, a computerised studio consists of an electronics engineer, a number of computer programmers, and some specialist designers who can also be animators, managers and promoters. Abel's company, Robert Abel Associates, works very much along this line. One of the former Associates is Bill Kovacs, a brilliant computer programmer who did some excellent three-dimensional computer-simulated work on synthetic motion. He works in close cooperation with Robert Abel, who is a designer with a good sense of adapting technical innovations. They came up with many good ideas, including a system which they call 'Connect the Dots', which packs electronic impulses so closely together they appear as a continuous line. This system is certainly useful to their clients, since it enables them to watch the text and the choreography of a commercial as it takes shape (in 'real time') before the final version of the work is completed. As well as this, the computer is able to store the choreography, which could be re-used or altered at any time in the future.

Parallel to advances being made in images, some interesting developments have been taking place with synthetic sound, especially with regard to the composition of music. One realises that the role of the music is a vital support for the moving image, no matter how it was made or what system had been involved in its production. The relationship is based on two factors. Firstly, music is also conceived in terms of progression through time. It has a beginning, an end and a progression within those extremes. Like animation, it is precalculated, detailed, and structured on an almost mathematical formula. Such an interdependence has intrigued artists since the invention of the soundtrack and many fine experiments were carried out

Above: Robert Abel's updated, computer-generated logo for Columbia Pictures

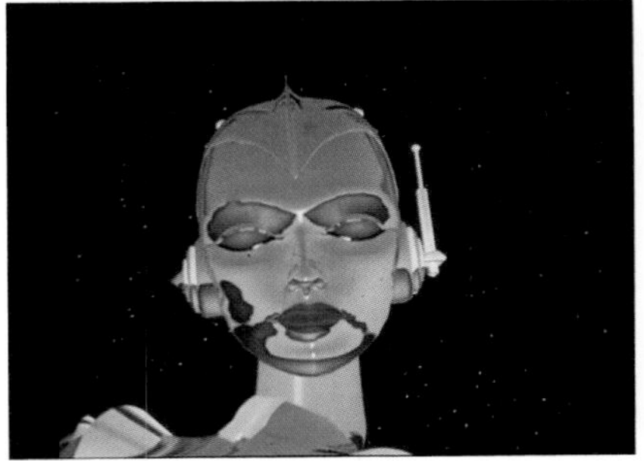

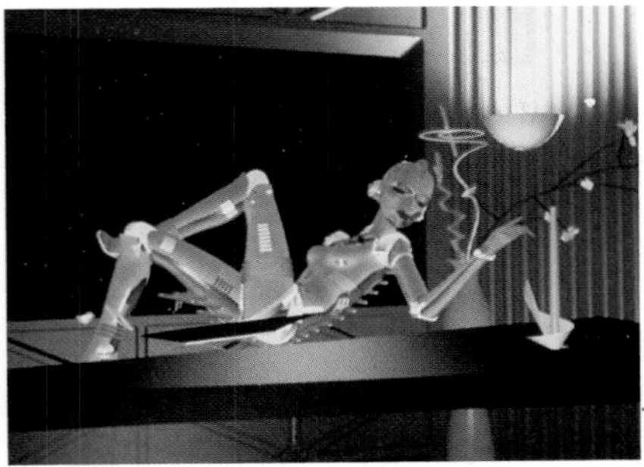

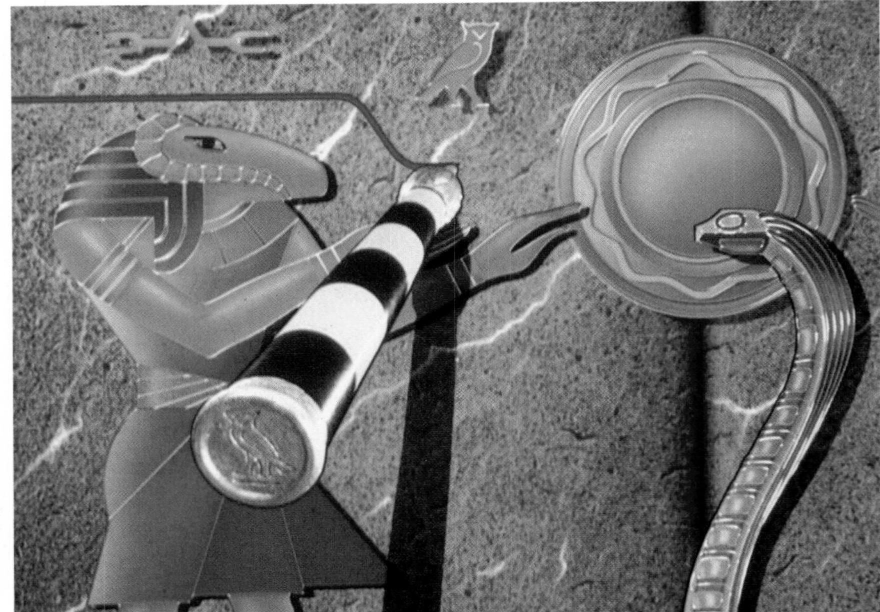

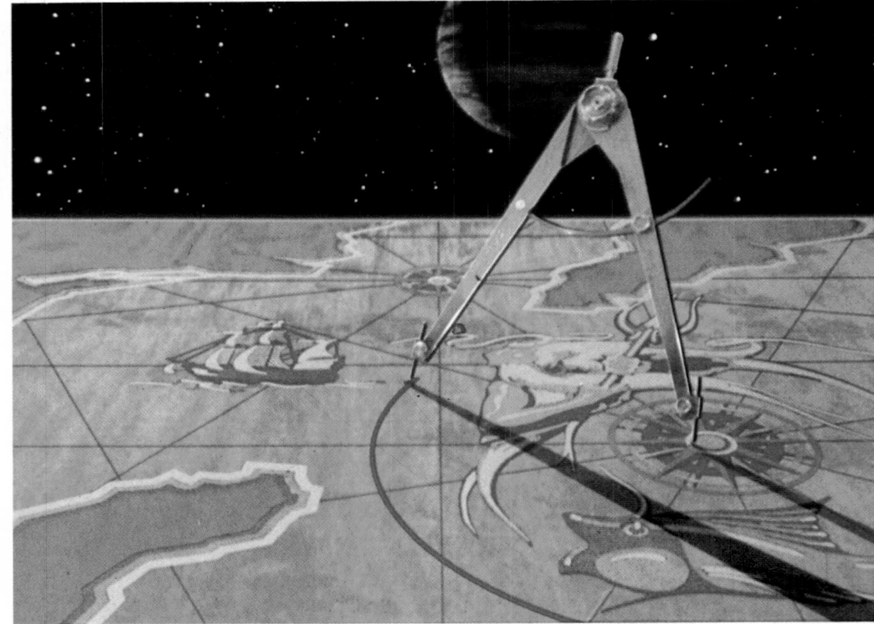

Examples of Robert Abel and his team's excellence in the field. Above: historical images, modern methods in *Line*; left: a sequence for Berger Paints; top: an innovative commercial for The Canned Food Information Council, *The Sexy Robot*.

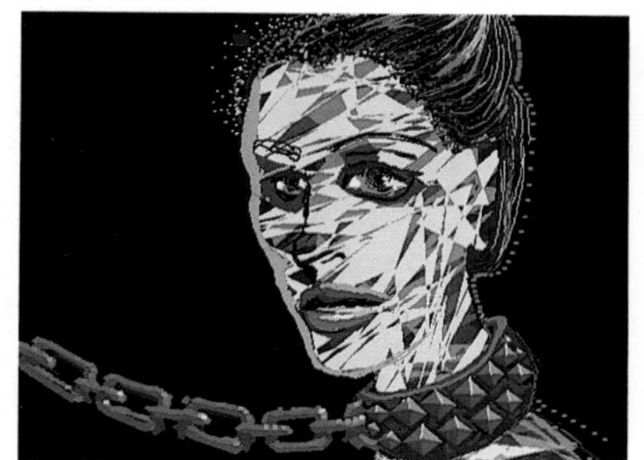

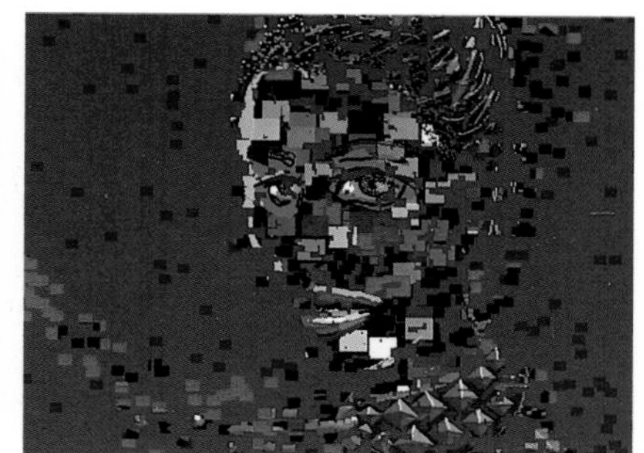

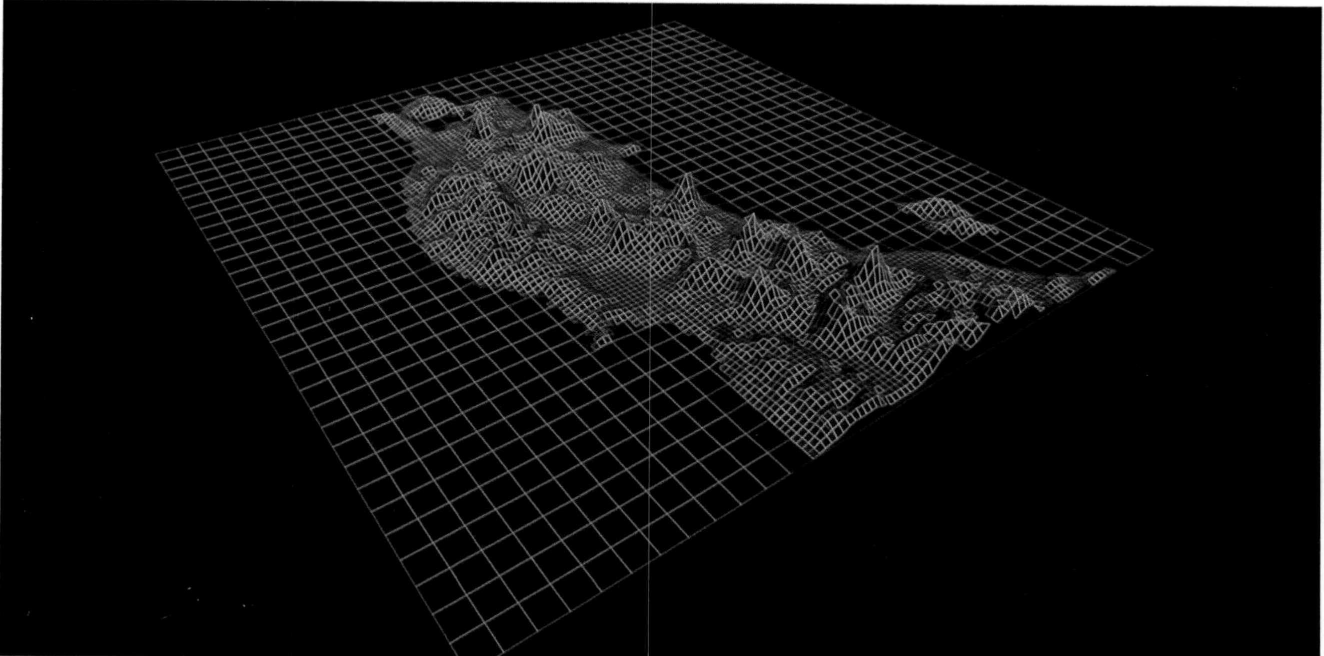

Work by Digital Effects Inc. Top: *Electric Lady* (Mark Lindquist and Judson Rosebush); above: *Power* (DEI/Japan); below: *Subway* (Mark Lindquist)

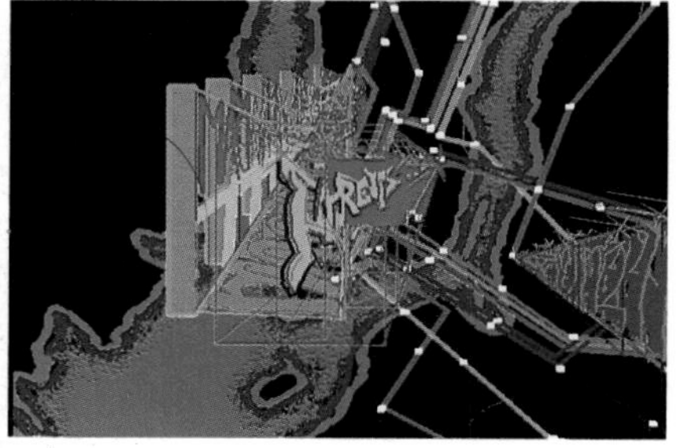

to prove what an added value the music could contribute. Today we are in a different phase of development in the relationship between the two elements. Computerised animation has a different look, a different feel to it, and it is important to be aware of this factor. Among others in Europe, Carter Burwell and Rebecca Allen (a computer animation director at the New York Institute of Technology) are experimenting with synthetic music tracks and plotting out the course of music electronically, which smoothly complements the electronic images. The process of marrying the levels of sound and image takes place via a time code and information on a tape for details of emphasis, in order to fit the animation to it later. This system has of course been used in productions of animated films for a long time, since for closer synchronisation it is usual to record the music and voice prior to animation. It is good to note that the problem of unity between computerised images and sound is now being tackled, as it does open up opportunities to experiment with sounds which have never been heard before.

In the hardware computer industry, the objective is to develop tools which can interact smoothly with the user. Out of this objective (on the way to producing the end product which is a television commercial on video tape) a number of new systems have come into existence. One of the latest and most useful computers is named Iris, which is the work of Silicon Graphics in the US. The problem to be solved was presented by advertising agencies who wanted a greater element of human identification in figure animation in television commercials than the mechanical look of most animated computerised characters. To endow three-dimensional robot figures with attractive or emotive qualities is, of course, a tall order, and a formidable challenge to computer artists. It is generally considered that the Abel team met the challenge successfully with the television spot for their client The Canned Food Information Council entitled *The Sexy Robot*. This may be the first incidence of a computerised character having strong audience appeal since my own experiment in the film *Dilemma* (see pages 83 and 119).

An active artist and computer animation expert is Judson Rosebush in New York. He has designed television station trademarks, contributed animation to the Disney production of *Tron* and designed exhibitions containing computer graphics. His strength lies in his ability to relate higher mathematics to computer languages, which enables him to work out special systems for his clients according to what type of equipment they have installed and how they want to apply it. Once again, it is difficult to appreciate the depth of his expertise without a thorough knowledge of computer jargon. Rosebush's list of services offered to his clients is generous, although it tends to be mystifying to those who know little about the profession. One of the facilities Rosebush offers is the Visions system, which is a three-dimensional interactive graphics software. It incorporates data management; object animation; perspective; light and shading; transparencies; shadows, and environment, image and texture mapping. Written in Fortran, the package allows users to define and manipulate images and show them on a Visual Display Unit as outlines or solids, with surface properties of colour, lustre, luminance, transparency and texture.

Also offered by Rosebush is the Video Palette III which is an interactive electronic paint system. It allows an artist to draw freehand with an electronic pen and tablet and view his or her work on a high resolution video monitor. The system requires no computer expertise and permits an artist to modify brush sizes, choose colours, and draw. Images can be repeated, magnified and stored, and colours can be mixed and saved.

Inevitably, as the production of computerised commercials expanded, so did the studios serving the market. Today there are some 250 computer graphic studios in the USA and Canada, as well as dozens in both Western Europe and Japan. Sogitec in Paris, for instance, have specialised in this field

Below: Art Durinski, setting colours and shading at the Omnibus computer animation studio in Hollywood; below right: the Antics studio at the Nippon Univac Information Systems, Tokyo, in 1985

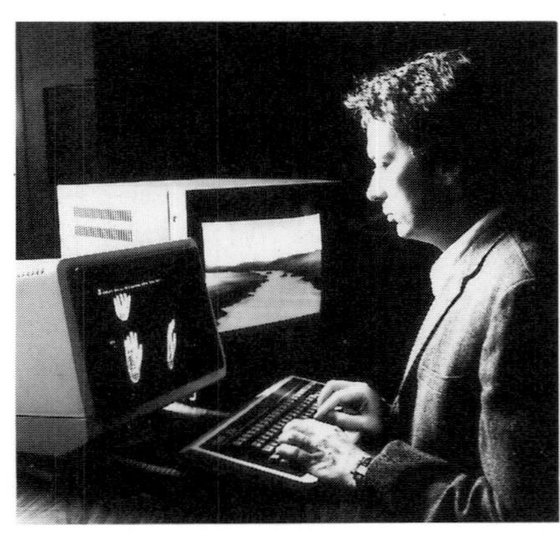

with a well-equipped studio. Their hardware includes the British-built Quantel Paint Box, possibly the world leader in paint systems. The opportunities created by the research department of the Institut National Audiovisuel in France are gradually being opened up to computer designers for commercials as well as other types of activities. Feverish activity is taking place in both Holland and Finland, where Antti Kari, in the Tööt studio, produced commercials and experimental computer graphic films. In Japan, the technology is rapidly providing new opportunities for artists like Masaki Fujihata, the highly talented Yukio Ota, Takashi Fukamoto and Toyohiko Higashi. The simplicity of Japanese design and their 'machine intelligence' is an excellent mixture for developing the computer graphics industry in that country.

As the list of the remaining masters of traditional animation is getting shorter, so the list of distinguished computer animators is getting longer and longer. In Britain, Bernard Lodge and Colin Cheesman, former designers with BBC TV, achieved an international reputation with a brilliantly-conceived television commercial for Panasonic. They are among the few who are able to achieve really innovative graphic design within the technical capability of computer tools. Talented scientists and innovators such as Dr John Vince at Rediffusion, who introduced the computer language 'Picasso', must also be mentioned, along with Stan Hayward, who teaches computer graphics at St Martin's School of Art in London. Tony Pritchett, an early pioneer in computer animation, has contributed programming to practically all computer-made films in Britain, and John Lansdowne has made some interesting computer films, including some excerpts for the animated feature film *Heavy Metal*.

Not new but notable for its durability is Alan Kitching's system Antics. Kitching has made many contributions to the development of computer animation, having that useful combination of technical knowledge and good design sense. With this background he was able to understand the artist's problem and developed Antics system to make graphic work easier on the computer. Like many other systems, the artist draws on an electronic pad with a light pen which can be used as freely as an ordinary one. Everything is explained in plain ordinary English: no computer knowledge is needed. Furthermore, drawings can be combined and animated in a variety of ways, providing an unlimited range of effects in full colour; thus an artist's personal style can be retained.

The value of Kitching's Antics system has been proved by the number of commercials produced in countries where the system has been installed, including the USA, Holland and Japan. The information production for the United Nations University in Tokyo is especially notable for its fluid animation and flexible computer graphics. Kitching started his experiments in London during 1973 and developed his hardware equipment and software computer system (ironically entitled 'The Stone Age Programme') on his own, without any institutional or official backing. He deserves his success.

For some time, just like professors of Biology or Mathematics who spend a lifetime studying their science, computer programmers tended to jealously guard their knowledge as private property. But slowly the locked doors are opening, and an important aspect of computer graphics is the part it is now playing in scientific and technical education. With the new tools, it is possible to reveal complex problems with clarity and simplicity. Evolutionary processes which have taken millions of years can be compressed into a few seconds; mathematical concepts previously inaccessible can be made crystal clear, and memory retention can be reinforced. Computer graphics are able to take learning processes a step further, especially with the storage capabilities and retrieval systems of a computer compared with oral or written material and facilities.

The medium is also, of course, extending over a wide field of other activities: computer graphics are now being used wherever visual communication is needed (see page 115). These activities are the more practical elements of the use of computer graphics, quite apart from its creative function as a tool for the animator. But these diverse activities are still waiting for a central connecting link between them. The next step, therefore, is to define a specific context for ideas and activities which did not exist before. If such a structure is found, computer graphics and computer animation could emerge as the most important communicating tools in our possession. However, in the process of looking for such a connection, a shift of emphasis must take place which concerns the role of the artist. In the future, the artist will have to become a strong force in developing a technology whose primary purpose will also be a medium for artists. That active engagement in this development holds the promise of involving many more artists, hitherto unable to utilise the medium because of the barriers imposed by the technological skills required. On this topic, Charles Sandbank, when he was Head of the BBC Research Department, remarked:

> 'The development of user/machine interfaces will have a major influence in our society in the next twenty years. Will we adapt to the computer or will the computer adapt to us? In the future we will no doubt see the combination of synthetic and camera images to their mutual artistic benefit as more directors become comfortable with the technology. Whichever way the major trend turns out, whether the computer will adapt to us or whether we will adapt to the computer, one thing is quite clear. Those who are willing to adapt to the machine, to the extent where they are capable of highly sophisticated interaction with the computer, will find this personally very rewarding and may well find themselves contributing to some of our most important future industrial cultural activities. These people should be encouraged and strongly supported. They are particularly important to us in Europe where this field provides a major challenge and an opportunity for the application of our wealth of imaginative innovation.'

Above: graphic transformation by Masaki Fujihata; opposite page, right: a Fujihata exploration into space, light, shape and mass

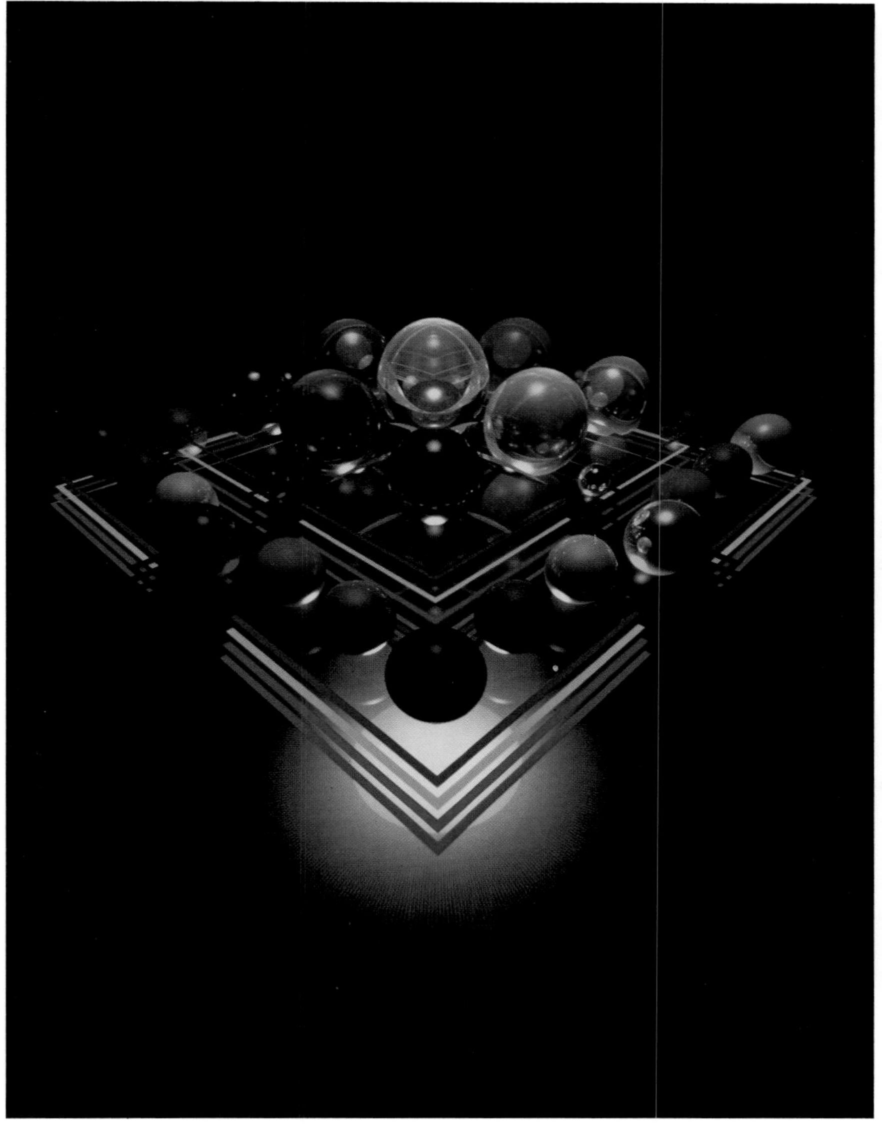

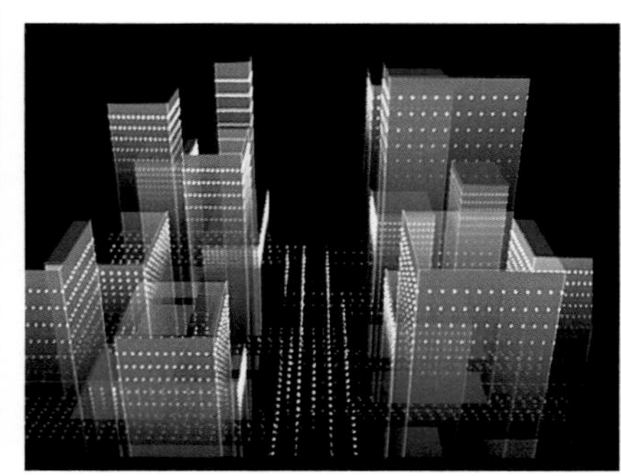

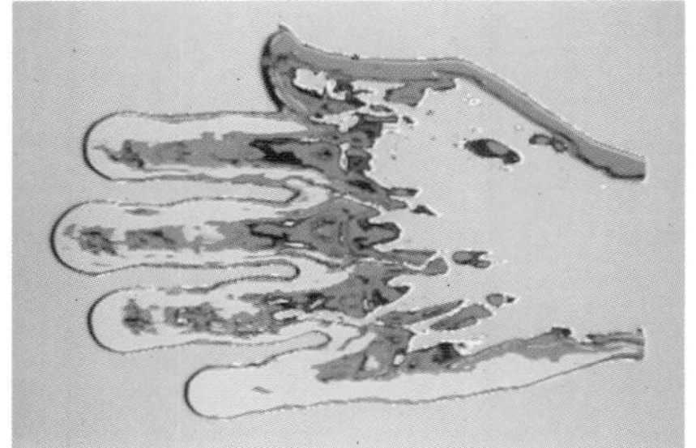

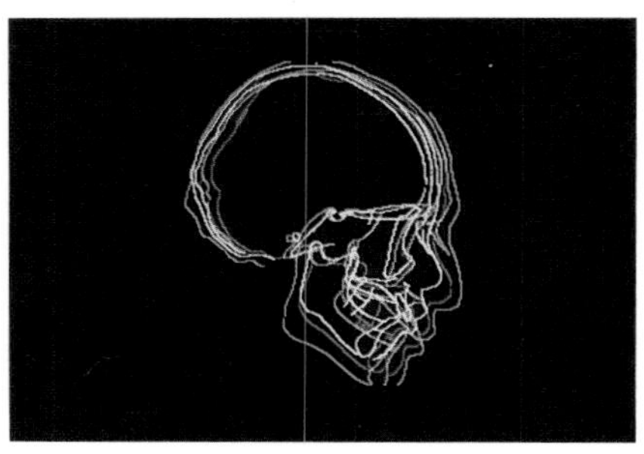

Left and far left: anatomical animation by Antics; above: *Skyscrapers* by Aoyama Computer School; centre: *30*, a commercial by Fumi Kaneko, NUIS; top: *SV3*, a Toyota commercial by Sig Sakai of Totsu Video Centre

CONCLUSION

As we have seen, animation is a truly international medium, practised by masters of the art in almost every developed country in the world. Indeed, many animated films can be appreciated by audiences everywhere, regardless of national or cultural barriers. A direct consequence of animation's universal appeal was the formation of the International Animated Film Association (ASIFA) in 1960. Animators from many different nations felt the need to take stock of the progress made since the international expansion of the medium. (ASIFA has since grown to include thousands of members; it has groups in fifty-six countries and works towards improving the status of animation and the prospects for its practitioners throughout the world.)

The decades leading up to ASIFA's emergence have been full of movement and change. After the medium took hold as a new form of entertainment at the beginning of the twentieth century, it went on to develop in many diverse areas. Advancements in the technical field (such as the introduction of the soundtrack) were inevitably accompanied by exciting artistic innovations; the exploration, for instance, of the fundamental relationship between visual and auditory impact, producing films like *Fantasia* in 1940.

After a period of technical development and artistic experiment, animation as a popular form of mass entertainment reached a peak with the highly sophisticated work of the Disney Studio in the forties and fifties. What many saw as a decline into an imitation of live cinema sparked off a revolt among animators who wanted the medium to reflect progressive treatments of graphic design and abstract forms.

It was around this time that television took over as the main exposure for animated cartoons, and just as the cinema had inspired favourite characters, so television soon produced its own. This was not simply a matter of a transplant from big screen to small: the vast difference in budgets for cinema and television meant that it necessitated something of a change in the genre. Nevertheless, television quickly became an established medium for the animated cartoon.

Undoubtedly the biggest transition animation has gone through, however, is the relatively recent widespread adoption of computer-generated techniques (see page 119). To a large extent, television encouraged this development, with its demands for programme titles, announcements and advertising. What is interesting is that the huge advance in the special effects made possible by computer animation has succeeded in putting the medium back into the cinema, in the shape of sophisticated science fiction features. Many of the films thus produced remind one of the early efforts by the pioneers of animated 'trick' photography. *Ghostbusters* (1984), for instance, has much in common with Blackton's *The Haunted Hotel* made in 1907 (see page 19). The actual techniques used for the former are much more complex, of course, and today's audiences can assimilate 'supernatural' images and effects much faster than audiences of the 1900s. The idea, however, is essentially the same and 'magical' illusions are created which are simply not possible with any other medium.

Moreover, just as with the early period of film-making at the beginning of the twentieth century, the creation of these films is once again in the hands of individuals; names like Méliès and Blackton having been replaced by Spielberg, Lucas and others. The production of these films obviously requires knowledge of the new possibilities and the tools, which include electronic pens, synthesisers and computers. Electronic painting, 'input and output monitor capacity', graphic display systems, 'vector modes', memory storage and a whole range of devices are necessary to create the contemporary moving image. For the newest generation of master animators, these tools provide additional means of expression, a significant enrichment for the medium, an expansion of its uses and the capacity to reach vast new audiences. Science and art have at last come together to produce the vital art form of the future.

BIBLIOGRAPHY · PICTURE CREDITS

★ *The titles or editions listed with an asterisk are out of print*

Adamson, J. *Tex Avery: king of cartoons* New York: Popular Library, 1975;★ New York: DaCapo, paperback 1985.
Andersen, Y. *Make your own animated movies: Yellow Ball Workshop film techniques* Boston: Little Brown, 1970.★
Arnheim, R. *Art and visual perception: a psychology of the creative eye* Berkeley: University of California Press, 1965;★ 2nd rev. edn 1974.
Blair, P. *Animation: learn how to draw animated cartoons* Laguna Beach, California: Foster, 1949.★
Cabarga, L. *The Fleischer story* New York: Crown, 1976.
Collins, M. *Norman McLaren* Ottawa: Canadian Film Institute, 1976.
Crafton, D. *Before Mickey: the animated film 1898–1928* Cambridge, Massachusetts: The MIT Press, 1982.
Edera, B. and Halas, J. (eds) *Full-length animated feature films* London: Focal Press, 1977.
Feild, R.D. *The art of Walt Disney: from Mickey Mouse to the magic kingdoms* New York: Abrams, 1973.
Halas, J. and Manvell, R. *Art in movement: new directions in animation* London: Studio Vista, 1970.★
Halas, J. (et al.) *Computer animation* London: Focal Press, 1974.★
Halas, J. *Design in motion* London: Studio Vista, 1962.★
Halas, J. and Herdeg, W. *Film and TV graphics* Geneva: Graphics Press, 1968.
Halas, J. *Film animation: a simplified approach* Paris: UNESCO, 1976.★
Halas, J. *Graphics in motion* Munich: Novum Gebrauchs-graphik, 1982.
Halas, J. and Manvell, R. *The technique of film animation* London: Focal Press, 1960;★ 4th edn 1976.★
Halas, J. (ed.) *Visual scripting* London: Focal Press, 1976.★
Hausen, R.H. *Film fantasy scrapbook* New York: Barnes, 1972.★
Heraldson, D. *Creators of life: a history of animation* New York: Drake Publications, 1975.★
Herdeg, W. *Film and TV graphics 2* New York: Hastings House, 1976.
Holloway, R. *Z is for Zagreb* New York: Barnes, 1972;★ London: Tantivy Press, 1972.★
Laybourne, K. *The animation book* New York: Crown, 1979.
Levitan, E. *Animation art in the commercial film* New York: Reinhold, 1960.★
Levitan, E. *Handbook of animation techniques* New York: Van Nostrand, 1979.
Lutz, E.G. *Animated cartoons: how they are made: their origin and development* London: Chapman and Hall, 1920;★ New York: Gordon Press, 1976.★
McLaren, N. *Cameraless animation* Ottowa: National Film Board of Canada, 1958.★
Madsen, R.P. *Animated films: concepts, methods, uses* New York: Interland, 1969.
Manvell, R. *Art and animation* London: Educational Film Centre, 1980.★
Muybridge, E. *Animals in motion* New York: Dover, 1957.
Muybridge, E. *The human figure in motion* New York: Dover, 1955.
Perisac, Z. *The animation stand* London: Focal Press, 1976.★
Salt, B.G.D. *Basic animation stand techniques* Oxford: Pergamon, 1976.
Salt, B.G.D. *Movements in animation* Oxford: Pergamon, 1976.
Solomon, C. and Stark, R. *The Complete Kodak animation book* Rochester, New York: Eastman Kodak, 1983.
Stephenson, R. *The animated film* London: Tantivy, 1973.★
Whitaker, H. and Halas, J. *Timing for animation* London: Focal Press, 1981.

Picture Credits

The author would like to thank the copyright holders of all material reproduced herein. The publishers gratefully acknowledge the following: The Science Museum (pages 12–13 (top), 14 (bottom), 15 (top), 17 (bottom)); La Cinémathèque québécoise, Montreal (page 16); The Museum of Modern Art/Film Stills Archive, N.Y. (page 17 (top)); Columbia Pictures Industries Inc. (page 36); Harvard University Art Museums (The Busch Reisinger Museum) Gift of Sibyl Moholy-Nagy (page 44 (bottom)); Albright-Knox Art Gallery, Buffalo, N.Y. Bequest of A. Conger Goodyear, Gift of George F. Goodyear (page 46 (top)). Every effort has been made to contact the copyright holders of material reproduced. The author would be grateful for any information regarding unacknowledged sources.

INDEX

Page numbers in *italic* refer to illustrations